DISCOVER · NATURE

in
Winter

DISCOVER · NATURE

in Winter

Things to Know and Things to Do

Elizabeth P. Lawlor

with illustrations by Pat Archer

STACKPOLE
BOOKS

Published by
STACKPOLE BOOKS
5067 Ritter Road
Mechanicsburg, PA 17055
www.stackpolebooks.com

Printed in the United States of America

Cover illustrations by Pat Archer

Cover design by Wendy A. Reynolds

10 9 8 7 6 5 4 3 2 1

First edition

Library of Congress Cataloging-in-Publication Data

Lawlor, Elizabeth P.
    Discover nature in winter : things to know and things to do / Elizabeth P. Lawlor : with illustrations by Pat Archer. — 1st ed.
        p.   cm.
    Includes bibliographical references (p.   ).
    Summary: Introduces common living things that continue to make a living during the winter and suggests activities for discovering what each creature looks like, where it lives, and how it survives.
    ISBN 0-8117-2719-X (alk. paper)
    1. Natural history—Juvenile literature. 2. Winter—Juvenile literature. 3. Nature study—Juvenile literature. [1. Natural history. 2. Winter. 3. Nature study.]
    I. Archer, Pat. ill. II. title.
QH48.L26   1998
508.2—dc21   98-17606
                                                                            CIP
                                                                            AC

This book is dedicated
to Heather and her kin,
whose disarming charms capture
the hearts of all who meet them

One touch of nature makes the whole world kin

—William Shakespeare

Contents

ACKNOWLEDGMENTS

Books of this nature are seldom the work of a single person. I consulted many experts in various fields of science and natural history, who willingly shared their knowledge with me. In the course of our conversations, they clarified many points and reconciled conflicting pieces of information sometimes found in the literature.

The people who helped me are Dr. Don Cox, Rice Creek Field Station, State University of New York, Oswego; Ted Gilman, Environmental Education Specialist, National Audubon Society Center, Greenwich, Connecticut; Amie Gallagher, Hayden Planetarium, Museum of Natural History, New York; Jena Guarino and Ned Swanberg, Vermont Institute of Natural Sciences, Woodstock; Dr. Steven Young, Institute of Northern Studies, Wolcott, Vermont; and Paul Rezendes and Paulette Roy, Programs in Tracking, South Royalston, Massachusetts.

I also thank Sally Atwater and Val Gittings for their continued patience and editorial skills, which have helped fine-tune my manuscrtipt. And finally thanks to Jane Devlin, associate editor, who continues the tradition of excellence at Stackpole Books.

INTRODUCTION

This book in the Discover Nature series is for people who want to find out about the wild things that thrive during the cold season. Like the other volumes of the series, this book is concerned with knowing and doing. It is for people who want to get close to nature. It is for the young, for students, for teachers, for parents, for retirees—for anyone with a new or renewed interest in the world around us. Getting started as a naturalist requires a friendly, patient guide; this book is just that. It is intended to gently lead you to the point of knowledge and experience where various field guides will be useful to you. When you have "done" this book, I hope that you will feel in touch with the creatures that live close to us during the winter.

Each chapter introduces you to common living things that continue to make a living during the harsh conditions of winter. Only those living things whose habitats cover a wide range and that are most easily found are included in this book. You do not have to live in a rural or wilderness area to find the plants and animals featured in this book. Most of the animals wander as close as your backyard, and the plants flourish in fields and meadows, along highways, and in parks. Each chapter also suggests activities you can do to discover for yourself what each creature looks like, where it lives, and how it survives.

The first part of each chapter presents the important facts about a particular living thing, including some amazing discoveries that scientists have made. The second part of each chapter, called "The World of . . .," guides you through a series of observational and exploratory activities. This hands-on involvement with plants and animals is the most important learning experience. This is how you will really discover what life in the winter is all about, something that you cannot acccomplish through reading alone.

HOW TO USE THIS BOOK

Feel free to start reading at any point in this book. If you're really interested in birds, for instance, and have a chance to observe them somewhere, read that chapter. Then read the section following this one, "What to Bring." You'll find additional items you'll need in the "What you will need" list in each chapter. This section will also tell you which specific science-process skills are developed in each activity. Do keep a field notebook. You can begin this process by making notes in the spaces provided in this book.

My great hope is that this book will be only a beginning for you. I have suggested other readings, keyed to each chapter, to help you learn more than this book can provide. In a sense, when you begin your explorations, you will go beyond what books can provide; Nature herself will be your guide.

WHAT TO BRING

To become fully involved in the hands-on activities suggested in this book, you'll need very little equipment. Your basic kit requires only a few essentials, starting with a field notebook. I generally use a spiral-bound, five-by-seven-inch memo book. Throw in some ballpoint pens as well as a few pencils, which are important as the ink in the pens is likely to freeze in very cold temperatures. Since several of the explorations will involve taking some measurements, a six-inch flexible ruler or a tape measure is another essential. Also include a small magnifier or hand lens. You may want to have a bug box—a small, see-through acrylic box with a magnifier permanently set into the lid. It's handy for examining small critters because with it you can capture and hold them for study, then release them unharmed; it also helps you examine seeds. A penknife is convenient to use to chip away bark from dead trees when hunting for evidence of insect life, and several small sandwich bags are also useful to have on hand.

All the basic kit contents easily fit into a medium-sized Ziploc bag, ready to carry in a backpack or the glove compartment of a car.

Basic Kit:
field notebook
pens and pencils
ruler
magnifier (hand lens)
bug box
penknife
small sandwich bags

Although not essential, a pair of binoculars adds to the joy of discovery when you are exploring. You might also like to take a camera and lenses for taking pictures of footprints in the snow or for photographing other finds on sunny days.

You may also want a three-ringed loose-leaf notebook in which to record, in an expanded form, the information you collect in the field. As you make notes, you'll have an opportunity to reflect on what you saw and to think through some of the questions raised during your explorations. Consult reference books and field guides for additional information. This more or less permanent notebook is an ideal place to keep photographs taken in the field.

As you read and investigate, you will come to understand how fragile these communities of living things can be. You will inevitably encounter the effects of man's presence. I hope you will become concerned in specific, practical ways. This kind of concern is the way to make a difference for the future of the environment.

PART I

THE SCENE

CHAPTER I

Winter

THE "WHYS" OF THE COLD SEASON

In ancient times, when people living in the northern latitudes watched the days grow shorter as the sun rose and set farther and farther to the south, the increasing darkness of the cold season brought renewed awe and the nagging fear that the sun would disappear and not return. Those people could never be sure that the sun would climb again in the sky and bring back the longer, warmer days of summer.

They didn't realize that the sun was not moving away from the earth as it appeared to be, because they lacked a mechanical understanding of the solar system. Today we have that understanding, and it has come to us through the collective efforts and observations of generations of philosophers and scientists.

Anthropologists tell us that for many thousands of years, people have been fascinated with the sky. Stonehenge, the huge circle of enormous stone slabs in southern England, was apparently erected to help predict the seasonal movements of the sun and moon. As long ago as 1400 B.C., American Indians also created rings of stone so that they could follow the movements of the sun and the stars. The Chinese, Babylonians, and Egyptians also contributed to our knowledge of celestial bodies. But it was the Greek astronomer Ptolemy who, in the first century A.D., invented a model of the solar system that made sense of day and night and of the seasons. He proposed that the earth was the center of the universe and that all heavenly bodies revolved around it. This geocentric theory, built on the observations of many others, had great appeal and survived for about fifteen hundred years. Although this theory began as a simple model, it gradually became more complicated as astronomers noticed what appeared to be an occasionally "backward" motion of the planets with respect to the stars.

In 1543, Nicolaus Copernicus upset the status quo when he theorized that the sun was the center of the universe and all other heavenly bodies revolved around it. Johannes Kepler added that the planets orbit the sun in ovals (ellipses) and not in circles as Copernicus thought. What this means is that at some point in their journey around the sun the planets are closer to the sun than at other times in their orbit.

About one hundred years later, Galileo observed several moons revolving around Jupiter. These observations gave solid proof that not all heavenly bodies revolve around the sun. Discoveries of distant galaxies that contain billions of stars have replaced the sun-centered concept of the universe with a model that shows our solar system as a tiny speck within the Milky Way galaxy, which in turn is a tiny smear among billions of other galaxies.

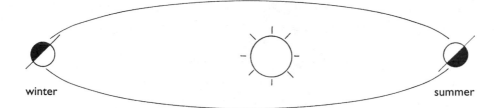

The axis of the earth is tilted at an angle of 23° to the plane of its orbit, and this causes the seasons. The earth is actually closer to the sun in winter.

What primitive people saw and explained through their mythology we now make sense of through these models. The Copernican model helps us explain seasonal changes as the earth makes its annual journey around the sun. The tilt of the earth on its axis is the entire explanation for the seasons. When the North Pole is angled away from the sun, the Northern Hemisphere experiences winter and the Southern Hemisphere summer. When the North Pole is angled toward the sun, the seasons are reversed. This explanation has nothing to do with the fact that the earth moves closer to and farther from the sun in its yearly revolution. At the winter solstice, the earth is approximately 91,406,000 miles from the sun, but in the summer, the distance away from the sun is 93,500,000 miles.

The only part of the earth not severely affected by the tilt on its axis is a band on either side of the equator. People living in these tropical regions do not experience winter.

The first day of winter in the Northern Hemisphere is around December 21. You might be surprised to learn that this date is not fixed, and in some years, winter occurs on December 22. You will need to consult an almanac to find out when winter will arrive in any given year. The first day of winter occurs when the sun appears at its most southerly position in the sky, appearing to be directly overhead at the position on earth called the tropic of Capricorn (23 degrees, 27 minutes south latitude). Although it is said that the first day of winter is the shortest day of the year, you will discover in the activities that follow that there are peculiarities about that day. A clue to one of these peculiarities can be found in the phrase "winter solstice." The word *solstice* comes from two Latin words: *sol,* meaning "sun," and *stice,* meaning "static" or "still."

Winter is a season of hardships for those who live where cold makes an annual visit. Although some people escape these hard times by migrating to warmer regions, most of us stay put; we simply add more wood to the stove or push up the thermostat, and when we venture outside we pile on an extra layer of clothing to conserve our body heat.

Plants and animals that don't migrate away from the cold season find winter difficult because of the bone-chilling cold. The shorter days of the dark season reduce the number of hours available for animals to forage, and the long nights strain the energy reserves acquired during the day. Snow cover makes it difficult for herbivores and carnivores alike to find food. The glaze of ice that may coat birds' wings and snap tree limbs presents another hazard of the season, but it's winter wind that delivers the most lethal wallop. It is the greatest danger to life that winter poses, because moving air accelerates heat loss from an inadequately protected body.

Anyone who has spent time outdoors in the winter knows that wind can make a cold day feel even colder. Normally your body produces a layer of warm air that insulates you against the cold. Proper clothing will keep this warm air close to your skin. When you are inadequately dressed, the heated air close to your body is replaced by the colder, denser air of the wind. Continual movement of the wind across your exposed skin accelerates the transfer of heat by steadily pushing the warmer, lighter air away and replacing it with the colder, denser air. This process is called convection and is the basis for the concept of windchill.

If the temperature drops to 10 degrees Fahrenheit and is accompanied by a twenty-mile-an-hour wind, it will seem to the unprepared traveler that the temperature is a chilling minus 25 degrees F. The harder the wind blows, the colder it will seem to be to skin that is exposed or covered only by thin clothing. You will feel cold whenever your body loses heat to the surrounding or ambient environment.

In addition to convection, three other physical processes are involved in heat loss: radiation, conduction, and evaporation. On a windless day, you can lose body heat through radiation. In this process, heat is transferred from a warm object to a cooler object by electromagnetic waves. Radiated heat is invisible to the naked eye but can be "seen" by special infrared cameras and detectors. We can detect these infrared radiations with our skin when we sit across the room from a blazing fireplace. The sun's heat stored in the wood reaches us indirectly through these radiations. On a cold day, you can lose as much as 50 percent of your body heat from a hatless head through radiation, because the scalp is richly supplied with warm blood. The greater the difference between the temperature of your scalp and the temperature of the surrounding air, the greater the loss of body heat. This is the science behind the conventional wisdom that you should wear a hat if you want warm feet.

Heat also may be lost through conduction. This happens when a warm body comes in direct contact with an object colder than itself. You have experienced conduction at work if you have ever sat on a rock or a metal conduit. It does not take very long for you to become aware of the cold seat. Heat may be lost through conduction from poorly insulated feet, and wet clothing will also conduct valuable heat away from your body.

Heat loss through evaporation occurs when the surface of your body becomes wet, usually through perspiration. Evaporation of this moistness will lower the skin temperature. Dry winter air and warm wet skin will produce a fast evaporation rate.

Living things have evolved many different strategies to help them survive the harshness of winter. Many life forms begin preparing for the cold season in late summer or early autumn. Signs of these preparations are all around us, but perhaps one of the most obvious is the flocks of geese and ducks that gather in northern fields and meadows in preparation for their southern migration. Songbirds such as common yellowthroats and wood thrushes depart for Mexico, Panama, or Guatemala in search of richer feeding grounds; bobolinks head for the Argentine pampas to celebrate another summer.

Animals that cannot escape to warmer climes survive the cold season by adjusting their physiology and behavior. Bats, woodchucks, and shrews hibernate, but most animals use other techniques to carry them through the season of scant food and freezing temperatures. Chipmunks store acorns and other nuts, which will supply energy when the cold comes. These animals den up. They fall into a torpor, a state from which they awaken periodically to feast on their caches of nuts. Deer use another strategy. They conserve their energy by moving very little, and they remain close to red maple saplings and other good browse.

Plants have developed various strategies for surviving the winter. Deciduous trees and shrubs shut down their energy factories and shed their leaves. Many wildflowers and other field and forest plant species survive the winter in the form of seeds that remain dormant until conditions suitable for germination return. Other plant species spend the cold season in the form of bulbs or underground stems. This method of producing new offspring without seeds is called vegetative propagation. With the coming of spring, new plants will arise from these structures.

THE WORLD OF WINTER

What you will need	Science skills
basic kit	observing
almanac	recording
local newspaper	comparing
graph paper	graphing
outdoor thermometers	
wind speed indicator	

OBSERVATIONS

Daylight Wanes. Day length is a measure of the number of hours and minutes the sun is above the horizon on any given day—that is, the length of daylight between sunrise and sunset. Keep a record of the number of daylight hours during the month of September. You can find the times of sunrise and sunset listed in your local newspaper. Record your information on a chart similar to the one below. Does the decrease in the number of daylight hours occur at regular intervals? What is the rate of change before and after the winter solstice?

CHANGES IN THE NUMBER OF DAYLIGHT HOURS DURING (MONTH)

Date	Sunrise	Sunset	Length of Daylight	Change Per Day (Plus or Minus)
9/15	6:49	7:17	12 hr., 28 min.	
9/16	6:50	7:15	12 hr., 25 min.	-3 min.
9/17	6:51	7:14	12 hr., 23 min.	-2 min.
9/18	6:52	7:12	12 hr., 20 min.	-3 min.
9/19	6:53	7:10	12 hr., 17 min.	-3 min.
9/20	6:54	7:09	12 hr., 15 min.	-2 min.
9/21	6:55	7:07	12 hr., 12 min.	-3 min.

Sample table for figuring changes in daylight. Based on sunrise and sunset figures given in Bob Ryan's Almanac and Guide for Washington D.C.

After you have figured out the change in the amount of daylight from day to day, make a graph of your findings. If you can follow the change in the

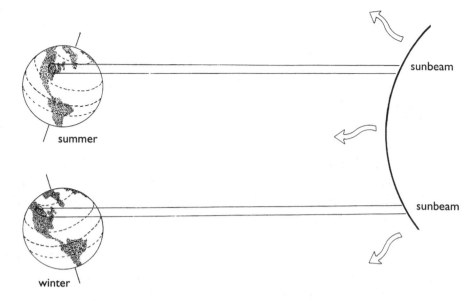

Winters are not warmer, even though the earth is closer to the sun. Since radiation is spread out because of the tilt of the earth away from the sun, a sunbeam must cover a larger area in winter, and the radiation is less per given unit area.

number of daylight hours from the autumn equinox in September to sometime past the first day of winter, you will have a record of the changing hours of daylight as the sun appears to move away from us and as it begins its apparent return.

What did you find out? For how many days does the "shortest day" actually last? (See Chapter Note 1.) When did you first hear people say they noticed the days getting longer? How does the perceived increase in day length compare with what is actually happening?

How many daylight hours are there in December? Compare this with the number of daylight hours in January, February, or March. How does the time of sunrise change as winter progresses? Is the pattern the same for sunset? Make a graph to illustrate these changes, but before you do, predict the "picture" the data will produce. How long does winter last? (See Chapter Note 2).

After the first day of winter, how do the times of sunrise and sunset change? By the end of January, how much has the length of daylight increased? By the end of February? You will need your local newspaper to figure this out. Continue monitoring the increase in daylight hours until the summer solstice in June. Make a graph for each month. What generalizations can you make about the changes in the number of daylight hours for this period?

Sunrise and Sunset. With the help of a compass, some simple observations will tell you that the sun sets directly in the west and rises directly in the east at the autumn equinox (September 23) and at the spring equinox (March 21). It is said that during the winter, the sun rises in a southeasterly direction and sets in a southwesterly direction. Do you find this to be true? How do the directions of the rising and setting sun change as winter progresses? (See Chapter Note 3.)

Winter Color. Although trees and flowers have lost their carnival hues of summer and autumn, the winter landscape has its own palette. To enjoy its subtle hues, you need to train your eyes to see them. Snow helps sharpen the definition of colors—greens appear greener, reds redder. Do you find this to be true with other colors as well?

How many different shades of green, gray, and brown can you find? Look for the pewter-colored bark of the beech tree and the red twigs of the red maple. The deep red of sumac berries (see Chapter Note 4) and the antique gold of meadow grass contrast exquisitely with the paper white bark of the gray birch. Look for the pale yellow of the winter sun reflected at sunset. What colors are present in a winter sunrise?

Make a chart in your field journal to display the colors of winter and the sources of those colors. Use the paint chips found in the paint sections of hardware stores to help sharpen your color sense. Explore as many different habitats as you can. Visit a winter meadow with or without snow cover, a woodland, a beach, a salt marsh, a dune system, a park, and of course, your own backyard and the street where you live.

Be sure to include birds in your survey. The bright red cardinals and blue jays brighten even the most dreary winter day. The black and white of downy and hairy woodpeckers are a sharp contrast to the subdued world, and the vivid red head markings of the males add a note of cheer. What other colors do birds bring to your neighborhood? What plants or animals provide the most color? (See Chapter Note 5 for clues on finding color during the "drab" season.)

Winter's Voices. Snow affects the way sounds travel. Without looking out the window, you can tell when there has been an accumulation of snow during the night because the ordinary sounds of the outdoors are muffled.

After a fresh snowfall, bundle up and go for a walk. Listen for the subtle winter sounds. Do you hear the moan of the wind in the pines, its gentle murmur in the hemlocks, the rattle of leaves still dangling on oak trees, the groan and creak of a pair of tree trunks rubbing together? Listen for the blue jay's raucous call and the cheery song of the chickadees. In late afternoon you may hear the whinny of a screech owl or the "Who cook for me?" question posed by the barred owl. Listen to the sound of your own breathing and the crunch of your footsteps on the snow.

Keep a record of the sounds you hear in your field journal. Record the location, time of day, and the date of your observations. Repeat the activity on another day when there is little or no snow on the ground and note the differences.

"The Days Lengthen, the Cold Strengthens." You can find out if there is any truth to this old saying by hanging an outdoor thermometer where it can be read easily. Record the temperature through the months of January, February, and March. At the same time, record the number of daylight hours for each day that you have a temperature reading. What relationship do you find between the temperature and the number of daylight hours?

RELATIONSHIP BETWEEN TEMPERATURE AND THE NUMBER OF DAYLIGHT HOURS

Date	Temperature	Number of Daylight Hours

How Cold Does It Feel? The presence of wind makes the outside temperature seem much colder. This phenomenon is called the "windchill factor." To determine the windchill, you need a cold, windy day, one or two outdoor thermometers, and a hand-held wind speed indicator, which you can buy at a marine shop for less than $10. How does the wind speed change when you hold the indicator at ground level and then over your head? Use a thermometer to find out the temperature of the air in both of these places. With the help of the accompanying windchill factor table, how has the wind changed the temperature?

Determine the windchill temperature in an open field and in a wooded area. Write an explanation of your discoveries in your field notebook.

How does the presence of a building change the windchill factor? On what side of the building is it the coldest? The warmest? How do the findings relate to the direction from which the wind is blowing? How do you explain the difference?

THE WINDCHILL FACTOR

Wind Speed (mph)	Thermometer Readings (°F)									
	50	40	30	20	10	0	-10	-20	-30	-40
	Equivalent Temperatures (°F)									
Calm	50	40	30	20	10	0	-10	-20	-30	-40
5	48	37	27	16	6	-5	-15	-26	-36	-47
10	40	28	16	4	-9	-21	-33	-46	-58	-70
15	36	22	9	-5	-18	-36	-45	-58	-72	-85
20	32	18	4	-10	-25	-39	-53	-67	-82	-96
25	30	16	0	-15	-29	-44	-59	-74	-88	-104
30	28	13	-2	-18	-33	-48	-63	-79	-94	-109
35	27	11	-4	-20	-35	-49	-67	-82	-98	-113
40	26	10	-6	-21	-37	-53	-69	-85	-100	-116
	little danger			increasing danger			great danger			

Lunar Month Names. Several American Indian tribes named lunar months (twenty-nine days, twelve hours, forty-four minutes, and three seconds), or moons, for events occurring in the natural world. December was known as the Cold Moon. It signaled the onset of winter, with its short, cold days and long, dark nights. January was called the Wolf Moon, because the cries of hungry wolves could be heard in the winter night. February was dubbed the Snow Moon, as angry winds pushed the falling snow into deep drifts. March, which marks the end of winter and the beginning of spring, was named Worm Moon, as earthworms frequently made their appearance during this month of melting snow and mud. What name would you give to each month?

CHAPTER NOTES

1. The winter solstice is that time when the sun ceases its southerly journey and remains still for a period of time. We refer to this solar event as the "shortest day," but in reality it continues for several days. The rate of change in the number of daylight hours varies according to the time of the year. The rate is highest about September 22 and March 22 and lowest about December 22 and June 22.

2. Winter lasts eighty-nine days, give or take some hours and minutes.

3. During the winter, the sun rises in a southeasterly direction and sets in a southwesterly direction. Throughout the winter months you will notice that at sunrise the sun appears to move progressively toward the east and at sunset toward the west.

4. Staghorn sumac is a straggle shrub that generally grows between 4 and 15 feet tall, although it may reach a height of 30 feet or more. Its name comes from the resemblance of its branches to deer antlers. The deep red berries that make up the upright cone-shaped fruit clusters are valuable food for many songbirds, grouse, pheasant, and mourning doves. The twigs and branches also nourish white-tailed deer and cottontail rabbits.

5. Here are some sources of winter colors to get you started:

WINTER COLORS

Color	Plant or Animal
Blue	Eastern red cedar berries
Coral	Bittersweet berries
Deep red	Staghorn sumac berries
Mother-of-pearl	Milkweed pods
Yellow	Lichen
Yellow	Evening grosbeak
Red	Male cardinal
Tan	Female cardinal
Silver	Thistle and goldenrod seeds
Dresden blue	Blue jay

CHAPTER 2

Snow

THE EARTH'S QUILT

As the first snowflakes of the winter fall like confetti from the heavens, many people celebrate the event by dusting off their skis, sharpening the runners of their sleds, or building a snowman. Others are content to get their first taste of winter by catching the feathery flakes on outstretched tongues.

Perhaps you celebrate the coming of the snow in a more contemplative way. You may wonder about the fact that no two snowflakes are alike. You may puzzle over how snowflakes form in the gray sky overhead, or what happens to the crystalline miracles after they settle on the earth. You might ask whether freshly fallen snow has the same properties as snow found in older drifts made earlier in the winter, or if snow crystals keep their shape until the spring thaw reduces them to meltwater.

If you are fascinated by snowflakes, you have joined the company of many scientists and philosophers. Long ago, Aristotle pondered the nature of snow. The seventeenth-century astronomer Johannes Kepler speculated on the six-sidedness of snowflakes. At about the same time, the French mathematician René Descartes published the first set of accurate drawings of snowflakes. Later, in the mid-1600s, the English scientist Robert Hooke first observed snowflakes under a microscope, which allowed snowflakes to be seen in greater detail. More recently, a Vermont farmer, William "Snowflake" Bentley, combined a microscope, a camera, and a lifelong fascination with snow to become an expert on these tiny jewels. His work (1865-1931) provided a vital source of information to scientists about snow formation and cloud seeding.

Snow crystals are born in high-altitude clouds tens of thousands of feet above the earth's surface, where the temperature is between 32 and minus 40 degrees F. The clouds are made up of water vapor in the form of fog or mist. They are composed of microscopic water molecules suspended in air. These water droplets are so small that millions of them could fit on the head of a pin. Clouds are visible because so many million trillion (quintillion) water droplets are concentrated in one area. When you walk through a fog or mist, you have had firsthand experience with a cloud.

Clouds form as rapidly rising air from the earth is quickly cooled. The water vapor it carries condenses around particles of dust; these are called condensation nuclei. These nuclei are essential to the formation of snow crystals because smooth-sided water molecules will slip by one another unless there is a solid, rough surface to hold them together. Although there is an abundance of dust in the atmosphere, only certain kinds of dust attract water vapor. The nuclei come from a variety of sources, such as tiny droplets of seawater that

How a snowflake is born

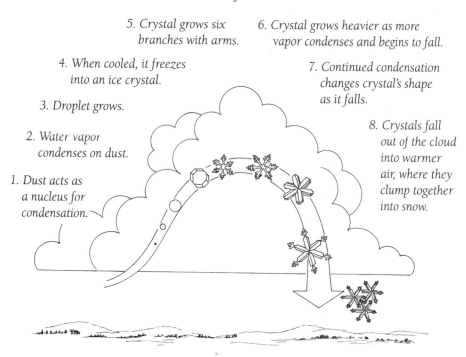

5. Crystal grows six branches with arms.

6. Crystal grows heavier as more vapor condenses and begins to fall.

4. When cooled, it freezes into an ice crystal.

7. Continued condensation changes crystal's shape as it falls.

3. Droplet grows.

2. Water vapor condenses on dust.

8. Crystals fall out of the cloud into warmer air, where they clump together into snow.

1. Dust acts as a nucleus for condensation.

fly from breaking waves and are carried aloft. The tiny particles of salt are lifted upward by air currents to act as condensation nuclei. Forest fires, smokestacks, automobile exhaust, volcanic eruptions, and even barbecues emit particles that will anchor water molecules to their surfaces. Soil particles in the atmosphere, such as clay, also serve as condensation nuclei.

Snowflakes are made up of very complex water (ice) crystals and can take on a seemingly limitless variety of forms. Scientists tell us that one tiny ice crystal is made up of one quintillion water molecules. Each molecule is triangular in shape and joins others to form a snowflake, which is always a variation of a six-sided, pointed star. It is this lattice or crystalline structure of ice that determines the fundamental six-sided symmetry of a snow crystal.

In 1951, the International Commission on Snow and Ice developed a classification system for snow crystals.

1. *Plates* are the most common form of ice crystals. These are six-sided crystals with a variety of intricate designs on their surfaces. They lack projections, and once formed, these "armless" crystals tumble freely through the atmosphere on their journey earthward.

2. *Columns* resemble six-sided hollow tubes with either flat or pointed ends. They are formed in very cold and very high-altitude cirrus clouds. During the winter, these crystals are responsible for the beautifully colored halos around the moon as the clouds pass in front of it.

3. Close relatives of columns are hollow *capped columns* that have plate crystals at either end of a six-sided hollow tube.

4. *Needles* are long, slender, six-sided crystals with pointed ends that readily combine with other ice crystals to form snowflakes.

5. *Spatial dendrites* are three-dimensional six-sided stars.

6. The star-shaped *stellar* or *dendrite crystals* are the classic image of a snowflake. The arms of the "star" radiate from the center and often have branches that form elaborate designs. Since their branches frequently interlock with other ice crystals, stellar crystals usually fall earthward as plump, conglomerate flakes. We see paper versions of these flakes decorating the winter windows of elementary schools.

7. The final group of snowflakes are those called *irregular.* Graupel is one of the many irregular snowflakes that belong to this catchall category. You may know the tiny, white, opaque ice particles of graupel as "soft hail" or "tapioca snow."

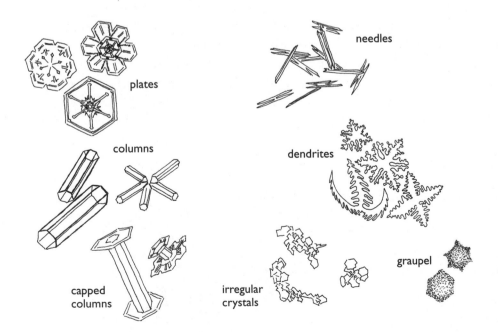

Categories of snow crystals

Although this system is useful to nonprofessional snow watchers, snow scientists have developed a more sophisticated system that uses eighty categories. With high-tech equipment such as scanning electron microscopes, scientists are now able to study minute details in snowflakes.

Snow scientists make a distinction between snowflakes and snow crystals. They regard snowflakes as clusters of individual crystals of frozen water. Snowflakes are born when snow crystals join together either as whole units or as broken pieces. A snowflake may be a fluffy mass with a diameter as large as three inches, whereas the largest snow crystal ever measured had a diameter of only a half inch.

Different types of snowflakes form at different temperatures. Based on ice crystal development under laboratory conditions, hexagonal plates form when the temperatures range from freezing to 27 degrees F. Plates with certain designs require temperatures to dip from 3 to minus 13 degrees F. Scientists produce needle-shaped crystals between 27 and 23 degrees F. The delicate fernlike stars develop at 10 to 3 degrees F.

The ice crystals that are elaborate in design generally form at relatively warm cloud temperatures when a generous supply of moisture is present. Smaller amounts of moisture produce smaller, simpler crystals. Redesigning occurs as a crystal falls and encounters air that is warmer than the crystal. Branches quickly develop and a new design is made.

Nearly everyone has heard that no two snowflakes are alike. Taking a new look at this old saw, scientists at the National Center for Atmospheric Research have studied the growth of crystals forming in high-altitude cirrus clouds, and in 1988 Nancy Knight accidentally found twins in samples of ice crystals that formed twenty thousand feet over Wisconsin. Snow scholars hesitate to call these snow crystals identical but are satisfied at this point to refer to them as "very much alike." The scientists remind us that in the twenty minutes or so that it takes an ice crystal to travel from the clouds to earth, two crystals would have to pass through identical conditions of temperature, pressure, and moisture content. They also would require identical collisions with other crystals. These collisions would have to cause identical splintering and fracturing of the ice crystals involved. The formation and re-formation of arms and smaller appendages would have to be identical. Finding two snowflakes that are identical in every aspect of their design is close to impossible.

Fallen ice crystals continue to change shape as they settle on the earth. The delicate arms and other protuberances that create the elegant designs are easily broken, and the spaces between ice crystals are reduced. The intricate design of an ice crystal results in a crystal that has a high surface-area-to-volume ratio. This condition is unstable. Partial melting reduces the ice crystal to a more stable round particle. The more elaborate the crystals, the more quickly they begin to change. Snow scientists call this process metamorphosis.

Eventually, warm spring air flows into snow country, causing the most dramatic changes to take place. Ice crystals melt, and this meltwater tumbles into brooks, streams, and rivers and cascades over rocks and fallen trees. It rushes toward bays and oceans, which are the spawning grounds for the next winter's snowflakes.

THE WORLD OF SNOW

What you will need	Science skills
basic kit	*observing*
thermometer	*recording*
coffee can or wide-mouthed jar	*inferring*
microscope and slides	*comparing*
clear lacquer spray	*measuring*
construction paper, assorted colors	
shovel	

OBSERVATIONS

Catching Snowflakes. Before you plan to catch snowflakes, put a piece of dark construction paper or fabric in the freezer. When it snows, place the frozen paper or fabric on a piece of sturdy cardboard for support, and allow the snowflakes to fall on the dark surface. Examine the snowflakes with a hand lens. Some snowflakes may look like fluffy pieces of lint; others may be ice crystals. Draw or describe the snowflakes you "caught" in your notebook.

A Closer Look. You will need a microscope and slides. A science teacher can help you secure these materials. You also will need a clear lacquer spray. Keep the slides and lacquer spray can in a freezer until you are ready to collect the snowflakes.

When the snow begins to fall, remove the slides and lacquer from the freezer and put them on a piece of dry cardboard that you have kept outside. This will prevent the heat from your hands from warming the slides and causing the flakes to melt.

Spray the slides with lacquer and carry them, on the cardboard, into the falling snow. After you have collected several snowflakes on the slides, put

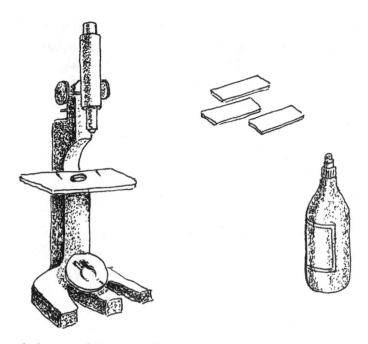

For a closer look at snowflakes, you will need a microscope, microscope slides, and clear lacquer spray.

them in a place away from the falling snow but still outside. Let them remain there for an hour or two until the lacquer has dried. Then, with the help of a microscope (forty power should work well), you can examine the imprints left by the snowflakes. Draw or describe them in your notebook.

Making a Snow Gauge. Weather reports often tell us how much accumulation we can expect from the next snowfall. You can make a snow gauge to find out how much snow falls in your neighborhood.

Tape a ruler to the inside of an empty coffee can. At the start of the next snowstorm put the container outside in an open area away from trees and buildings. When the storm ends, check the ruler to find out how much new snow there is. Is it the same amount the weather reports predicted, or is it more or less? Repeat this investigation for each snowstorm. How much snow falls each time? What is the total accumulation for a week? A month? The winter season? How does the total winter snow accumulation compare with that of last winter? Two years ago? Five years ago? The librarian at your local or school library can help you locate this information.

Record your findings in your field notebook. Make a graph of your discoveries. If you continue your observations of annual snowfall, you may be able to see some patterns. For example, which winter month generally has the greatest amount of snowfall? Which has the least? Keep records for several years. Does the greatest amount of snow fall during the same month each year?

How Pure Is the Driven Snow? Although you know that snow is made of water, have you ever wondered what else those elegant snowflakes carry as they slowly tumble earthward? To find out, perform this simple test.

Place a clean coffee can or wide-mouthed jar in an open space during a snowstorm. When the storm has ended, bring the container indoors where the snow will melt. Put a piece of filter paper, such as a coffee filter, into a kitchen funnel. Slowly pour half of the meltwater from the snow through the filter. What remains in the filter after the water has seeped through it? Examine the particles with a hand lens.

With a microscope, slides, and cover slips, you can examine the meltwater more closely. If you do not own these items, you can take the samples of meltwater to school and examine them there. Compare the remaining half of the meltwater with the filtered water. Write your observations in your notebook.

Snowpack and Temperature. On a very cold winter day, use a shovel to expose a cross-section of accumulated snow. Insert a household thermometer horizontally into the drift at a depth of about one or two inches. After three minutes or so, remove the thermometer and read the temperature. Record it. Repeat the procedure at the middle of the pack and at the base. What did you find out about the temperature related to the depth of snow? What implications does this have for animals struggling to survive the winter months?

Take readings early in the morning, at noon, and at sundown to find out what changes in temperature occur during the day. What did you find out?

Repeat these investigations in other areas around your neighborhood. Get some friends to do this with you. Then make a chart to display your findings.

TEMPERATURE PROFILE OF SNOWPACK

Temperature at Regular Depth Intervals	Location						
	1	2	3	4	5	6	7
4 in							
8 in							
12 in							
16 in							

EFFECTS OF TIME ON TEMPERATURE
AT BOTTOM OF SNOWPACK

Time of Day	Location						
	1	2	3	4	5	6	7
Early morning							
Noon							
Sundown							

Winter's Insulation. Snow is a good insulator and can protect plants and animals from deadly cold. Snow doesn't create heat; it holds what heat is released from the ground. The temperature under the snow at ground level may be a "cozy" 33 degrees F while the air temperature dips below zero. You can perform a simple test to find out how much protection is provided by about twelve inches of snow. Use an outdoor thermometer to measure the temperature of the air above the snow, then the temperature of the ground. Repeat this for several days. What did you find out? Would deeper snow offer greater insulation? Does the quality of the snow affect the insulating properties? Record your results on a chart such as the one provided here.

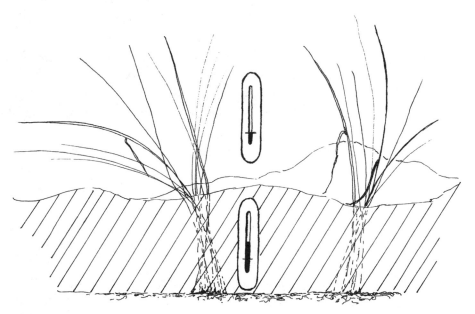

Pushing a thermometer into a snowdrift proves the insulating capacity of snow.

INSULATING CAPACITY OF SNOW

Day	Air Temp	Ground Temp
day 1		
day 2		
day 3		
day 4		
day 5		

Layers in a Snowpack. Find an undisturbed snowdrift and use a shovel to slice through the snowpack. How many layers are there? Are some layers thick and others thin? What are some possible explanations for the differences in thickness? (See Chapter Note 1.) Are some of the layers dirty and others clean? Are some layers icy? Where in the drift profile are the icy layers located? What do you think caused these different layers to form?

Examine the weather pages of local newspapers to determine when the different layers were formed. If more than one newspaper reports the weather in your area, is similar information provided by each newspaper?

Snow Produces Water. After a snowfall, fill a measuring cup with fresh snow and let it melt, then pour the meltwater into a measuring cup. Keep track of how many cups of snow it takes to make one cup of water. Repeat the investigation for old snow from the middle and bottom of a snowdrift. Does the amount of snow required to make a cup of water depend on the age of the snow? Do you need more or less snow if it is newly fallen? Old snow from the middle of a snowdrift? From the bottom of the snowdrift? (See Chapter Note 2.) Record your results in your notebook.

Snow Melt and Trees. Look for bare spaces around tree trunks and other dark objects when the rest of the ground is covered by snow. Dark objects absorb more heat than light ones. During the day, the tree absorbs heat from the sun. The tree radiates heat and melts the snow. What are the advantages of this to birds and animals living in that habitat? What other objects in your environment create similar bare spaces around them?

Color and Snow Melt. For this experiment, you will need same-size squares of construction paper in a variety of colors. Find an area where the snow cover is evenly distributed over flat ground. On a bright, sunny day, place all of the pieces on the snow, and leave them there for at least three hours.

Predict which square will sink the deepest into the snow. Which do you think will sink the least? Rank the colors in order of their "melt capacity." How accurate were your predictions?

Snow melts more quickly around trees and other dark objects.

COLOR AND SNOW MELT

Color	Predicted Rank	Inches below Snow Surface	Actual Rank
Red			
Yellow			
Green			
Dark blue			
Pale blue			
Black			
Tan			
Brown			
Orange			
White			

Now repeat the procedure using different pieces of materials such as aluminum foil, unpainted wood, wool, cotton, ceramic tile, linoleum, carpet, and Styrofoam. Be sure all the pieces are the same size. Which material sinks the deepest? Measure to find out.

The next time you see some old brown leaves that have sunk into the snow, explain to a friend why that happens.

Melt Rate of Snowballs. Get several different types of materials of uniform size that you can use as a surface on which to put your snowballs. The materials could include roof shingle, glass, cardboard, and any of those used in the previous experiments. On which surface do you predict the snowballs will melt the fastest? Rank the surfaces in order of their melt power. Now make several snowballs of equal size and test your predictions.

Which material melted the snowball fastest? Slowest? Why was the melt rate faster on some surfaces than on others?

MELT POWER OF MATERIALS

Material	Predicted Rank	Actual Rank
Wood		
Aluminum		
Shingle		
Glass		
Cardboard		
Styrofoam		

Temperature and Snow Melt. Does the temperature of snow change as it melts? You can find out by recording the temperature of the snow during the melting process. Pack a 4-ounce paper cup with snow. Invert the cup on a table and gently squeeze out the snow so that you get an upside-down cup-shaped heap of snow. Record the temperature of the snow every two or three minutes. Make a graph to show your results.

TEMPERATURE AND MELTING SNOW

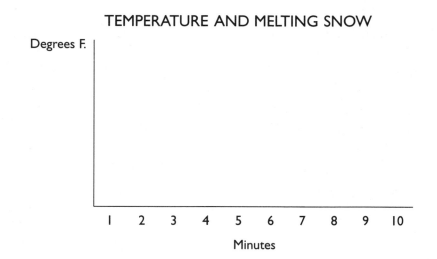

Dripless Snow. Make a snowball. Push a pencil into it. With the help of a lump of Playdoh, stand your snowball upright. How long does it take to begin melting? Put a similar-sized ice cube into a strainer. How long before the cube begins to melt? Compare with that of the snowball. (See Chapter Note 3.)

Repeat the experiment with several snowballs placed in different locations such as under a conifer, on the north and south sides of your house, and in an open area. Enlist some friends to help you and use stopwatches to find out how long it takes each snowball to begin melting. Record your findings in your field notebook. Why do you think the melt time varied from one place to another? Did sunlight, shade, or wind contribute to the melt time?

CHAPTER NOTES

1. In a snowpack, some layers will be thick and others thin. This happens because different amounts of snow may have fallen during different storms, and recrystallization may have taken place in the lower layers.

2. Newly fallen snow is fluffy and loosely packed. It will take about ten cups to make one cup of water. Snow within the drift is packed by the weight of snow above and by recrystallization of snow within the pack. You need only three to five cups of denser snow near the ground to make one cup of water.

3. A snowball melts more quickly than an equal quantity of water frozen into an ice cube because the snowball has more surface exposed to the air. In fact, air even circulates within the snowball unless it's very densely packed.

CHAPTER 3

Winter's Sky

ORION'S DOMAIN

It is easy to exerience the joys of winter. One of those joys is a quiet stroll on a cold, moonless night along a country road where the atmosphere is free from the glow of city lights and pollution. On such a night, the velvet, black sky is bejeweled with a dazzling array of stars. Winter, with its longer hours of darkness, is ideal for stargazing. Also, the winter sky is much clearer than in other seasons, as the air contains fewer dust particles and droplets of moisture.

If you have ever watched the sky as night approaches, you probably noticed that this spectacular display begins with the appearance of a few bright stars. Slowly, more and more stars dot the blackening dome overhead, and before you know it, thousands upon thousands of glittering jewels fill the heavens. There are so many stars strewn throughout the sky it seems impossible to count them.

Stargazing probably began when the earliest people looked at the night sky and tried to make order out of the jumble of stars they saw. Written records of stellar observations date from about three thousand years ago, when students of the night sky were shepherds, desert nomads, and farmers. These folks spent a great deal of time outdoors, and just as we see faces and animals in the clouds, they pictured things that were familiar to them in the star groups overhead. It is no surprise that they populated the sky with animals such as dogs, bears, fish, and lions. They also placed hunters and a legendary queen among the celestial cast of characters.

The ancient Greeks and Romans incorporated these star patterns into their myths, and artists made elaborate illustrations to represent them. Although these fanciful drawings can be found in books on mythology and astronomy, even the most inexperienced stargazer knows that reasonable facsimiles of these characters are nowhere to be seen in the night sky. For example, the legendary queen Cassiopeia appears in the ancient star maps complete with flowing robes seated on an elaborate throne, but the constellation of Cassiopeia consists of just five prominent stars in the shape of a W or a relaxed M, depending on the season. As centuries passed, the elaborate pictures gave way to outline sketches that resemble "connect-the-dot" pictures. Today astronomers use a grid system divided into degrees, minutes, and seconds of arc to find their way around the heavens. This relatively new technique retains the old constellations to identify particular areas of the starry sky. This system includes not only the familiar stars of a particular constellation, but also stars and galaxies within the area that are visible only by telescope. Because of this new mapping strategy, each of the traditional eighty-eight constellations identifies a parcel of sky, and each constellation looks more like a piece of a jigsaw puzzle than like the fanciful figures of years gone by. We will use the term *constellation* to refer to the more familiar patterns of stars that make up a character or object such as Orion, the Hunter, or Taurus, the Bull.

Of the trillion or more stars in the heavens, the most familiar is our sun. This fiery ball is a medium-sized star with a diameter of almost a million miles and a gravitational force strong enough to keep eight or nine planets (many astronomers do not consider Pluto to be a planet) in orbit around itself. Stars produce light through nuclear reactions in which hydrogen is transformed into helium. All heavenly bodies that produce light from such explosions are classified as stars. The explosions that result from these reactions keep the stars' internal temperature extremely high, anywhere from a relatively cool 3,800 degrees F to a relatively hot temperature of about 90,000 degrees F.

The temperature of a star and its color are related. When a blacksmith begins to join two pieces of metal with a torch, the color of the metal changes from a blazing red to blue-white or white as it heats up in the welding process. Similarly, the color of a star reflects its temperature, red stars being cool, blue-white ones hot.

The temperature of a star is also related to its age. Old and maturing stars are cooler and are red-orange to red; relatively young stars are hotter and are blue-white or white. On the road to maturity, white stars will ultimately become yellow, orange, and finally red. You can witness the results of the aging process by comparing two stars in the constellation Orion, which is prominent in the winter sky and easy for beginning stargazers to find. (See "Winter Constellations" below for instructions on how to find Orion.)

On the right shoulder of this celestial hunter is the bright galactic giant Betelgeuse. The volume of this old red star is about 200 million times that of the sun. In *Secrets of the Night Sky,* Bob Berman writes that if Betelgeuse were a jar and you were to put balls the size of the earth into it at the rate of one hundred per second, it would take you more than thirty thousand years to finish the job!

In Orion's left foot is another stellar giant, Rigel, a young, brilliant blue-white star nearly twice as far from the earth as Betelgeuse. You can find Rigel by tracing a line diagonally from Betelgeuse and passing beneath the hunter's three-star belt. (Although Rigel appears to be rather dim in comparison with Betelgeuse, astronomers say that Rigel is actually the brightest star in the constellation, and that it would take more than 50,000 to 60,000 suns to equal the brightness of Rigel.)

The brightness of stars does not necessarily indicate their closeness, however. Except for our sun, the stars are so far away that astronomers measure their distance in light-years. Light travels about 186,000 miles per second, and a light-year is equal to the distance light travels in one year in a vacuum, or about 5.88 trillion miles. A star's distance from the earth in light-years represents the number of years it takes light from that star to reach the earth. Rigel is about one thousand light-years away from us; Betelgeuse lies about 300 light-years from the earth. Rigel would cast shadows on the earth's surface if it were as close to earth as Sirius, the Dog Star, which is fifty light-years away.

Another characteristic astronomers use to classify stars is their relative brightness as we see it. In 1603, the astronomer Johann Bayer developed a system by which the apparent brightness of a star in a constellation can be described by assigning it a letter from the Greek alphabet. Using this system, the brightest star in a constellation is known as the alpha star and the second brightest is the beta star. Stars that are less bright are assigned Greek letters that reflect their relative brightness within a constellation. For example, the star called gamma Orini lets us know its home (Orion) and its relative brightness (the third brightest). The dimmest star in a constellation is the omega star, or the twenty-fourth along the continuum from bright to dim.

Using this system, Betelgeuse is called alpha Orini and Rigel is beta Orini. As you might expect, there are exceptions to this tidy rule, but these will not affect your enjoyment of the night sky. (See Chapter Note 1.)

When you look at Orion, you might get the impression that all of the stars are the same distance away and exist in the same plane. In reality, however, the stars that make up this constellation exist at vastly different distances from the earth. For example, Betelgeuse is about 300 light-years away from us, whereas Bellatrix, the star in Orion's left shoulder, is 510 light-years away. Mintaka, the most western star in Orion's belt, is about 1,467 light-years away, and Alnilam, the middle star in the belt, is still farther away, at 1,630 light-years. So in actuality, there is no such place as Orion.

This is true of other constellations as well. The stars Castor and Pollux, found in the constellation Gemini (The Twins), are close neighbors in astronomical terms, but one is closer to us by a dozen or so light-years. This is not at all close when we consider that light travels nearly six trillion miles in one year.

For travelers many years ago, the constellations were their sky maps. And today, even with radio and optical telescopes linked to computers housed in elaborate observatories, astronomers still use those ancient landmarks when they investigate the heavens. Even though the constellations assigned in the past may not completely suit the mathematical advances of our time, the scientists who study stars still make reference to those familiar formations. What would the winter sky be without the mighty hunter Orion and his faithful dogs?

THE WORLD OF THE WINTER SKY

What you will need	Science skills
basic kit	observing
binoculars	recording
flashlight with red filter	comparing
tape recorder	classifying
star maps	
compass	
small lump of modeling clay	

The cold, crisp evenings of late December, January, February, and early March are excellent for stargazing. Although there are many beautiful constellations and stars that you can observe with unaided eyes, using a pair of binoculars will add to your enjoyment.

OBSERVATIONS

Seeing in the Dark. Unlike owls and other nocturnal creatures, our eyes are not well designed for seeing in the dark. After leaving a lighted building at night, it takes about thirty minutes for our eyes to become adjusted to the lower light levels.

You can test the effectiveness of this process by making some observations. What can you see in the sky immediately after leaving the lighted building? What can you see after your eyes have become adapted to the dark? Are you able to see more stars? If you know some of the constellations, can you see stars inside the constellations that you did not see before your eyes adjusted to the dark? Make a journal entry for each set of observations, but don't use a bright light to make notes. A good way to record your observations and still preserve your night vision is to use a tape recorder.

The Celestial Sphere. The term *celestial sphere* refers to an imaginary spherical shell that astronomers use to describe the relative positions of the moon, the sun, the stars, and the planets. In this model the sky is a hollow

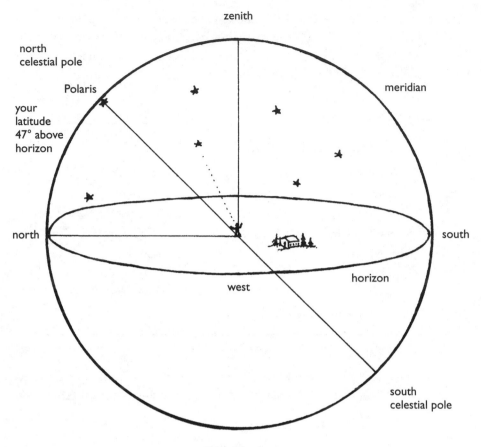

Celestial sphere

ball with the earth suspended at its center, and the stars are "glued" to the inside wall of the sphere. This model is not a replica of the sky-earth relationship, but it provides us with a tool that helps us understand the apparent daily and yearly movement of the stars relative to the earth.

Note in the illustration that the earth's equator is projected onto the celestial sphere. This projection is known as the *celestial equator.* Similarly, the projected North and South Poles become the *north celestial pole* and the *south celestial pole.* Stars near the celestial poles never set for observers in the midlatitudes of the Northern and Southern Hemispheres and are visible throughout the year. To find out how this works, you will need a small lump of modeling clay (the "observer") and a globe. Place your observer at the North Pole. Spin the globe. As the globe spins, you can see that the stars over the observer's head would seem to make circular paths in the sky. If your imaginary observer were to take a photograph of the night sky, he would produce a print of the circumpolar constellations similar to the illustration.

No matter where you are on earth, you will be able to see only half of the celestial sphere. Therefore, what you see in the night sky is partially determined by your location. Use your globe and the clay observer to see how this works. If you are observing the sky from New York or any place around 43 degrees north latitude, for example, the domelike section of the sky you see is the northern portion of the celestial sphere.

Locating Stars. You may want to help a friend find a particular star. To do this, you do not have to be a mathematics wizard, but you will both need to know some terms.

Go outside into an open area and face north (use a compass if necessary). The point directly over your head is called the *zenith*. The place in front of you where the earth and sky seem to meet is called the *horizon*. If you live in a hilly area, your horizon will be jagged, but if you live in a flat area, your horizon will be fairly straight.

The *altitude* of a star is the number of degrees it is up from the horizon. A star directly overhead (at the zenith) has an altitude of 90 degrees; a star halfway between the horizon and the zenith has an altitude of 45 degrees. The *meridian* is an imaginary line that extends from the north horizon through the zenith to the south horizon. It divides the sky into east and west sections. The *azimuth* of a star is measured in degrees around the horizon like the points of a compass. The north point on the horizon is 0 degrees. If you are facing north, your right side will be pointing 90 degrees, or due east. Directly behind you is south, or 180 degrees, and left of you is due west, or 270 degrees. The North Star will always have an azimuth of 0 degrees and an altitude corresponding approximately to your latitude.

Star Movement. Every twenty-four hours, the earth rotates counterclockwise on its axis, from west to east. This rotation causes the stars, sun, and moon to appear as though they move in a great arc across the sky from east to west. For observers in the United States, stars and other heavenly bodies that pass near the zenith seem to move in half-circles as they rise, cross the sky, and set. Stars to the south seem to scribe smaller arcs rather than half-circles. Stars to the north, especially those close to the North Star, make circles overhead. The closer the stars are to the poles, the tighter the circles they make (see illustration).

Only those constellations that pass overhead at night are visible to us. In the winter months, these include Gemini, Taurus, Orion, the Great Bear (Ursa Major), the Little Bear (Ursa Minor), Leo, Boötes, and Virgo.

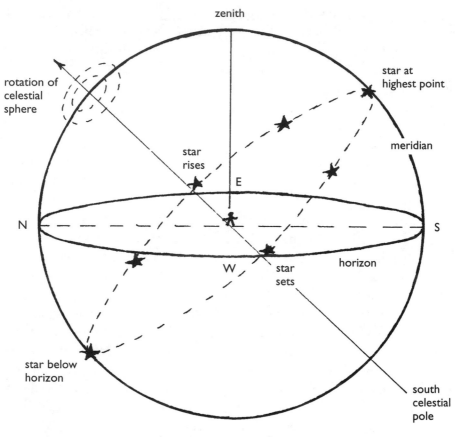

Apparent movement of a star

Star Rise. Stars do not rise and cross the sky and set at exactly the same time every night; they rise and set four minutes earlier each night. In fifteen days, they will rise and set an hour earlier, and in thirty days, two hours earlier. As the months go on, those stars that you saw initially in the western sky at about 9 P.M. will not be visible at all; they will cross the sky after sunrise. This is why different constellations are overhead at night at different times throughout the year.

Zodiac. The fact that the earth is rotating and orbiting the sun creates the appearance that the sun, moon, and planets are moving nightly and yearly across the starry sky. As the year progresses, they appear to pass through twelve of the constellations, known as the constellations of the zodiac. This interesting illusion gave rise to the twelve signs of the zodiac so popular with the mythology of astrology. Astrology is based on astronomical beliefs that were common before the development of the telescope and modern theories

THE SCENE

of astronomy. On any particular day, the sun, moon, and planets each appear to be in one of the twelve zodiac constellations. Followers of astrology can use charts to determine in which of the twelve the sun, moon, and certain planets were located on their date of birth. You can use the daily newspaper to find out which is your zodiac constellation. Use a star map to see what this constellation looks like. At what time of year is it visible in your area? What are the major stars in your constellation?

Universal Changes. The stars are in constant motion, but you will not notice any change in the position of the stars relative to one another. They are so far away from us that individually they do not appear to be moving at all. The illustration shows how the stars of the Big Dipper have changed their relative positions over a period of millions of years, as well as what the Big Dipper may look like in the distant future. The constellations as we see them are temporary and illusory star patterns valid for just a brief period in the vast expanse of time. Some archaeologists believe that ancient structures like the Egyptian pyramids were built to aim an observer's eye toward stars that have moved out of the stone "viewfinder" over the centuries.

Circumpolar Stars. The circumpolar stars and constellations are those that revolve around Polaris, also known as the North Star or polestar, like spots on a record spinning on a turntable. The illustration represents a time-lapse photo of the path these stars follow when viewed directly overhead. These stars neither rise nor set. They are constantly turning overhead, even when they are hidden from our view by sunlight. In the Southern Hemisphere, there is no visible star located so conveniently. A time-lapse photo in the Southern Hemisphere would also show circular star paths, with a piece of empty sky at the center.

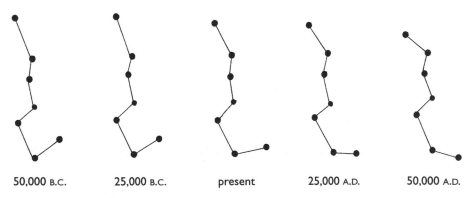

| 50,000 B.C. | 25,000 B.C. | present | 25,000 A.D. | 50,000 A.D. |

The changing form of the Big Dipper

A one-hour time exposure facing due north would show this much motion in the stars. Polaris is the dot in the center.

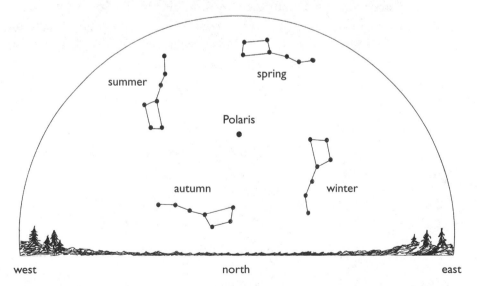

west   north   east

Observing the sky about 9 P.M., you will see that the Big Dipper circles around Polaris from season to season.

You can see the circumpolar stars from anywhere in North America on a cloudless night. Your location on the earth will determine where in the sky you will see these stars. If you live in Alaska or northern Canada, the circumpolar stars will appear almost directly overhead; if you live in the southern states, these stars will appear close to the horizon. Use the instructions below to find the North Star. Put a camera on a flat spot outdoors on a dark, clear night to make your own star-track photos. The shutter must remain open for at least ten or fifteen minutes. An hour or more is better.

Winter Constellations. Each season of the year has its own set of constellations. With a little practice you will be able to identify these star patterns. You can use the constellations to locate additional stars in the winter sky.

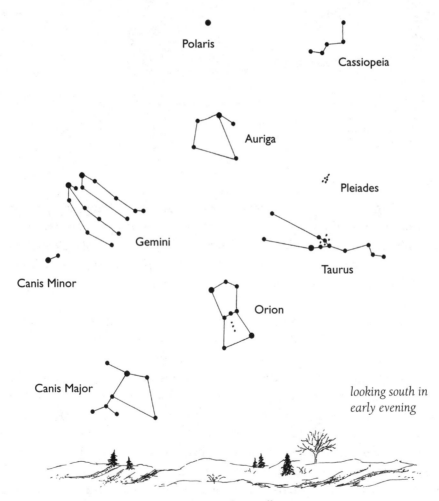

Winter stars and constellations

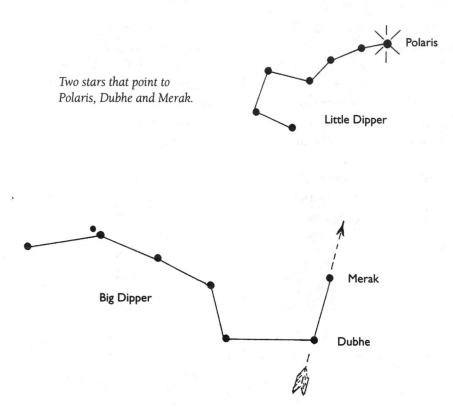

Two stars that point to Polaris, Dubhe and Merak.

Polaris

Little Dipper

Merak

Big Dipper

Dubhe

The Big Dipper. Almost everyone recognizes the seven stars conspicuously arranged in the shape of a very large scoop or dipper in the northern sky. This well-known landmark, the Big Dipper, is a good place for you to begin your study of the stars. Although often referred to as a constellation, astronomers call this group of stars an asterism that is within the Great Bear constellation.

Seven major stars form the Big Dipper. Look for the curved handle of the dipper and the four stars that make its bowl. The "pointer stars," Merak and Dubhe (pronounced "Dubby"), are the two bright stars that form the outer side of the dipper's bowl. If you draw an imaginary line up (away from the horizon) from them to the nearest star that is moderately bright, you will have reached the North Star. Don't be surprised that it is not very bright. Polaris is a magnitude 2 star, important but not glamorous.

The North Star has guided navigators throughout the millennia. This is an important star, because the northern end of the earth's axis is pointed toward it. This places it almost directly above our geographical North Pole. It is an important navigational star, even with today's high-tech navigational equipment. The other polar constellations turn in a great circle around Polaris, as though it were the hub of a wheel. What do you think the Big Dipper would look like when viewed from the North Pole? (See Chapter Note 2.)

The Pleiades. This cluster of stars, frequently called The Seven Sisters, is part of the constellation Taurus. You can find the cluster if you draw an imaginary line from the star that marks Orion's left shoulder and pass it through Aldebaran, which is also located in Taurus. Continue the line to the cluster of stars beyond Aldebaran and you will reach the Pleiades. For a special treat, look at them with a pair of binoculars.

The Great Bear (*Ursa Major*). This circumpolar constellation is made up of the Big Dipper and other stars. After you have located the Big Dipper, look for the stars that form the Great Bear. The handle of the dipper is the bear's tail, and the bowl of the dipper contributes to the bear's back. Can you find the bear's head and front legs? Use the accompanying illustration as a guide, but make your own drawing in your notebook. Don't forget to identify compass directions in your notes.

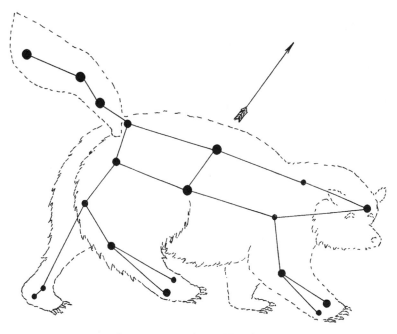

The Great Bear (Ursa Major)

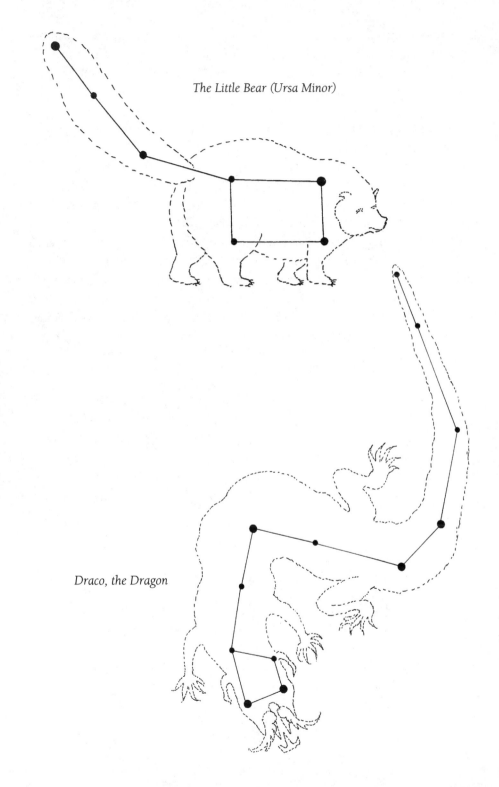

The Little Bear (Ursa Minor)

Draco, the Dragon

The Little Dipper. The stars that form this group are part of a larger constellation called the *Little Bear (Ursa Minor)*. As in the Big Dipper, there are seven stars. Four stars make the bowl, and three form the curved handle. If you follow the line of the handle stars, you will find a small and lonely star. This is the North Star.

Because all the stars of the Little Dipper are small and faint, it is not as easy to find as the Big Dipper. If you remember that the Little Dipper appears as though it were pouring something into the Big Dipper, it is easier to find. Again, don't confuse this with the Pleiades. In your notebook, make a drawing of this star group. Compare the positions of the dippers with each other at 8 P.M. in January, February, and March. What did you notice?

Draco, the Dragon. This is a long, sprawling line of stars that begins with an irregular diamond that forms the dragon's head. Look for the last two tail stars, which are about ten degrees (one fist width) from the pointers of the Big Dipper. They are of equal brightness and lie between the cups of the Big and Little Dippers. Draw an imaginary line from the tail stars in the direction of the handle of the Big Dipper, making an arc below the Little Dipper, until the line of stars ends at the dragon's head.

Cassiopeia. The queen's chair is found on the other side of Polaris from the Big Dipper. Find Alioth, the third star in from the handle of the Big Dipper. Draw a line from Alioth to Polaris. Draw another line of equal length from

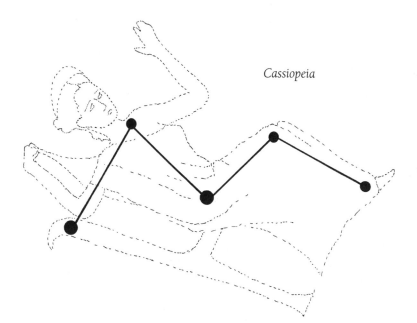

Cassiopeia

Polaris to a group of stars of equal brightness that are in the shape of a relaxed upside-down W or an M. You have found Cassiopeia, or Cassiopeia's Chair, as the constellation is sometimes called.

Cepheus. Look between Draco's head and Cassiopeia, and you will find Cepheus. It looks like a rectangle wearing a dunce cap. Don't be discouraged if you have trouble finding Cepheus, because it is not as easy to locate as the other circumpolar constellations.

Orion. Orion, the hunter, seems to consume the southern region of the sky. This constellation is so dominant that we often describe the location of other stars relative to it. Look for the mighty hunter early in the evening. The three bright stars in his belt (magnitude 2) are easy to find. Two widely separated stars above the belt mark his shoulders, and two similarly separated stars below the belt mark his arms and legs. A curving line of stars hanging

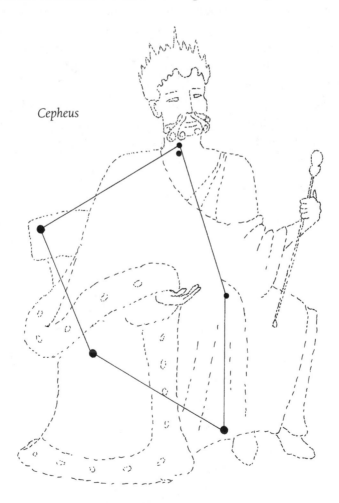

Cepheus

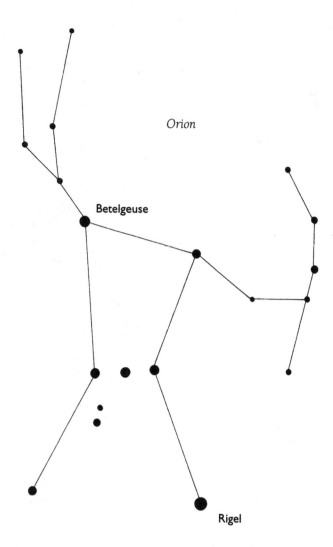

Orion

Betelgeuse

Rigel

obliquely from the belt form Orion's sword. Orion's sword contains a hazy region called the Orion Nebula. In this area of gas and dust clouds, new stars are forming. You can see the nebula with a pair of binoculars.

Betelgeuse is the only bright, orange star in the constellation. To find it, look above and to the left of the belt. It marks Orion's right shoulder. If you look an equal distance below the belt, you will find another bright star, called Rigel, forming the left foot. These two stars illustrate star evolution. Betelgeuse is an old star burning red like the embers in a tired campfire, and Rigel burns in the blue-white heat of youth.

The stars in the constellation of Orion can help you find your way around the winter sky. Use the map on the next page as a guide to the landmarks.

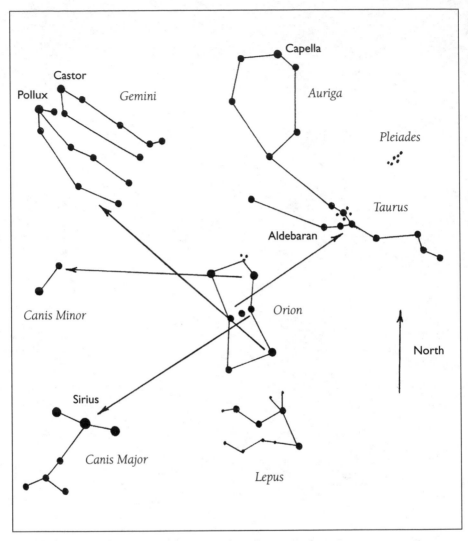

Orion as a guide to the winter sky

Canis Major. You can find this constellation by tracing a line southeast from Orion's belt to Sirius, the Dog Star. Sirius is the brightest star in the constellation, and astronomers say it is the brightest star in the heavens (magnitude -1.6).

Canis Minor. A line drawn west from Betelgeuse to the next bright star will bring you to Procyon. This is usually the only visible star in the constellation Canis Minor. Canis Major and Canis Minor are Orion's two faithful dogs that follow the hunter across the winter sky.

Taurus, the Bull. Draw a line northwest of Orion's belt the same length as the line to Sirius, and you will find a V-shaped group of stars. These are in the constellation Taurus, the bull. Aldebaran is the brightest star in the constellation and burns bright red.

Gemini. A line from Rigel through Betelgeuse will bring you to Castor and Pollux. Look for these matched stars directly overhead. (With the help of larger, more powerful telescopes, astromoners have learned that Castor is really a stellar system made up of seven stars.) Although they appear to be

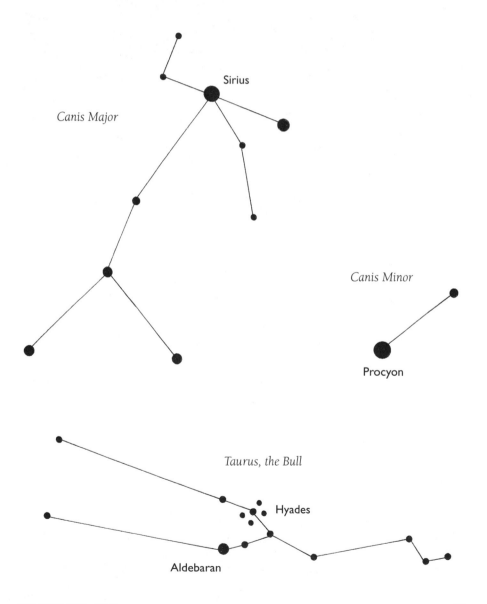

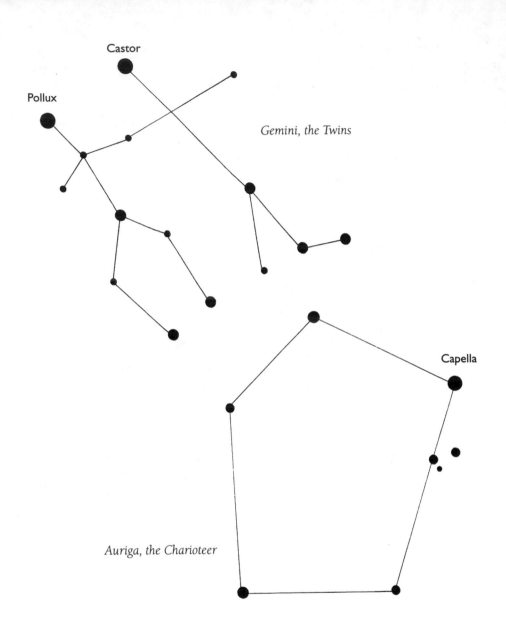

Castor

Pollux

Gemini, the Twins

Capella

Auriga, the Charioteer

close to each other, they are separated by eleven light-years. Castor is about fourteen light-years farther away from us than Pollux. Pollux is brighter and is the more southerly.

Auriga, the Charioteer. To locate this five-sided constellation, draw a line northward between Betelgeuse and Aldebaran. The brightest star in this group is Capella. It glows a bright yellow.

Find the Altitude of a Star. You can determine the altitude of a star if you remember some simple equations. 1. A fist held at arm's length equals ten degrees. 2. Three fingers are about equal to six degrees. 3. A pair of binoculars with a seven-degree field of view (7° marked on the binocular case) shows a seven-degree circle of sky.

Determine Your Latitude. The altitude of the North Star will give you your latitude. Sailors once used the North Star to navigate across the ocean on a particular line of latitude. They just kept on a course that put Polaris at the same angle above the northern horizon night after night.

Planets. The ancient stargazers discovered that some points of light in the night sky were not like the great majority. These points of light often did not twinkle. Some were very bright, others fairly dim. All of them had strange movements that were very different from regular stars. They all moved along the zodiac in erratic but predictable paths. They were a great puzzle and were called planets, meaning "wanderers."

Ancient astronomers had no idea that Earth was also a planet. They did come to realize that the planets were closer to Earth than the stars but farther away than the moon, because the moon blocked out light from the planets on rare occasions, and the planets could block out light from certain stars. The stars never blocked out each other's light. The ancients gave these wanderers the names of important gods—Venus, Mercury, Mars, Jupiter, Saturn—and attached great importance to their changing positions in relation to the zodiac constellations.

Look for Venus or Mercury low in the western sky around the time of sunset. These planets are so bright that they can often be seen before sunset and may be the first of the evening stars or the last of the morning stars. The daily newspaper often lists what other planets are visible in the night sky.

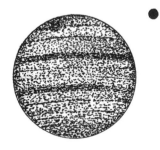

Jupiter, with the four largest of its sixteen moons.

Find Mars, the red planet, named for the god of war, who is associated with the blood of warriors. Mighty Jupiter, the foremost of the ancient gods, is also the largest of the planets. Look for Jupiter's four moons, visible through binoculars. The sight shocked Galileo and convinced him that Copernicus was correct: Earth is not the center of the universe, or even of the solar system! This discovery changed his life and nearly got him killed. With a pair of binoculars, look at the four moons of Jupiter for several nights. Each night make a sketch of what you see. (See Chapter Note 3.) Spotting Saturn with its rings in your binoculars is more difficult because this planet is dim, but it is a thrilling sight.

Why Stars Twinkle. If you look carefully, you will notice that the stars twinkle. Each of those twinkling bodies is a sun made up of 99 percent helium and hydrogen. The light from the atomic combustion of these gases travels to the earth. During the trip, the light from the burning gases is bent, rebent, and bent yet again as it passes through the stormy hot and cold air of our atmosphere. It is this bending that makes stars appear to twinkle. Astronauts in orbit don't see stars twinkling.

Planets are much closer to the earth than the stars are. Their relatively steady shine results from light reflected from our sun. This light makes them look more like glowing disks than shimmering points of light.

Star Color. Not all stars are yellow. As you spend some time stargazing, you will begin to notice variations in star color. Although it is possible to see the different colors of stars with the naked eye, a pair of binoculars will help you get a better view. Look for red, orange, yellow, and blue-white stars. The chart below lists the stars of some constellations and their colors. You can include any additional stars you find.

STAR COLOR

Color	Star	Constellation
Orange-red	Aldebaran	Taurus
Orange	Kochab	Little Dipper (the lip)
Red	Betelgeuse	Orion
Bluish white	Sirius	Canis Major
Bluish white	Rigel	Orion
White	Castor	Gemini
Yellowish	Pollux	Gemini

Winter Constellations and Stars. Use a chart to keep track of the constellations and their stars. Record the date and time of each sighting, along with any thoughts you might have. Record the directions you would give to a friend so that he or she could find the star or constellation. You can describe the altitude of the star as "almost overhead," "halfway up," or "low in the sky." Can you find the alpha star in each constellation?

WINTER CONSTELLATIONS

Constellation	Date	Time	Altitude	Directions
Ursa Major				
Ursa Minor				
Big Dipper				
Little Dipper				
Draco				
Cepheus				
Cassiopeia				
Orion				
Canis Major				
Canis Minor				
Taurus				
Gemini				
Auriga				

WINTER STARS AND STAR CLUSTERS

Star or Star Cluster	Date	Time	Altitude	Directions
Betelgeuse				
Rigel				
Capella				
Castor				
Pollux				
Procyon				
Sirius				
Pleiades				

CHAPTER NOTES

1. Brightness. To answer the question "How bright is that star?" scientists have devised two systems. One system of indicating relative visual brightness ranks stars that are visible to the naked eye within each constellation. According to this system, the brightest star in a constellation is given the label alpha, the next is beta, then gamma, and on down through the Greek alphabet.

GREEK ALPHABET

α	1	Alpha	ι	9	Iota	ρ	17	Rho
β	2	Beta	κ	10	Kappa	σ	18	Sigma
γ	3	Gamma	λ	11	Lambda	τ	19	Tau
δ	4	Delta	μ	12	Mu	υ	20	Upsilon
ε	5	Epsilon	ν	13	Nu	ϕ	21	Phi
ζ	6	Zeta	ξ	14	Xi	χ	22	Chi
η	7	Eta	$\o$	15	Omicron	ψ	23	Psi
θ	8	Theta	π	16	Pi	ω	24	Omega

A more modern labeling system assigns a relative brightness value to every star using magnitude numbers. Magnitude 1 stars, like Spica in the constellation Virgo, are 2.5 times as bright as magnitude 2 stars, such as Polaris. Magnitude 5 stars are barely visible to the naked eye and are 100 times as dim as magnitude 0 stars. Higher-magnitude stars are visible only in increasingly larger telescopes. Magnitude 29 stars are just barely visible with the Hubble space telescope. These stars are 250 billion times as dim as magnitude 0 stars. Including both Northern and Southern Hemispheres, there are about six thousand stars in the sky over the course of the year that are visible to the human eye.

2. If you were to view Polaris from the North Pole you would see that a line drawn from the end stars of the bowl (Merak and Dubhe) would always point to Polaris and that the handle of the Big Dipper would always point

toward the horizon. In this position the Big Dipper would scribe a circle overhead.

3. The four large moons of Jupiter that you see are named Io, Europa, Ganymede, and Callisto. As you follow their travels around Jupiter from night to night, you will see a change in their relative positions to Jupiter and to each other. Sometimes you will see all four moons on one side of Jupiter or two on each side. One may be invisible. This happens because each moon travels in its own orbit and at its own speed. Io orbits Jupiter in just under two days, but Europa takes three and a half days to go around the planet. Ganymede makes the trip in a week, and Callisto takes about seventeen days to complete its journey around Jupiter.

PART II

THE LIFE

CHAPTER 4

Birch Trees

OUR NATIONAL TREASURES

One of the most beautiful sights in the New England winter landscape is the birch tree. The trees are especially beautiful when the January sun plays a symphony of light on their unique white bark sheathed in ice. The word *birch* is derived from a word meaning "bright," "to shine," or "white." Members of the birch group grow almost everywhere in the Northern Hemisphere, but in the Northeast they are a regional symbol. In this part of the country, birches are featured in travel brochures and on postcards. They are frequent subjects for the artist's brush and the poet's pen. New England native Robert Frost skillfully captured the supple and resilient nature of birches in the much loved poem that bears their name. In *The Song of Hiawatha,* Longfellow tells us how Native Americans built sturdy, lightweight canoes from the bark of these trees. Some tribal groups used the bark of the white birch to keep a pictorial record of their history. In fact, President Thomas Jefferson recommended to explorers Lewis and Clark that they make a copy of their reports on durable birch bark, a suggestion they did not follow.

Birch is a genus of trees and shrubs that represents about fifty species. They are widely scattered throughout the temperate regions of the Northern Hemisphere, where they can grow to a height of thirty to eighty feet. You also can find birches in the subarctic regions, but this harsh climate severely stunts their growth. Tiny birch trees that eke out a living on thin arctic soil and are whipped by vicious winds grow to only a few inches in height.

Although there are many types of birch trees, we will look at the five native species that grow east of the Mississippi and across Canada from the Maritime Provinces to Alaska. As you begin to explore their world, you will find birches thriving in a variety of habitats, from sun-drenched fields to the moist lowlands of slow-moving rivers. Birch trees also are favorite plantings of homeowners and landscape gardeners, so you probably can find one in your neighborhood.

These trees delight the beginning tree sleuth, because the white bark that distinguishes two of the most widespread species makes them easy to identify as birch trees. There is no mistaking the white, or paper, birch (*Betula papyrifera*) and the gray birch (*Betula populifolia*). As you shall see, it is not difficult to tell which is which.

The white birch, diva of the north woods, has the most extensive range of all birches. Its graceful curves and white bark contrast sharply with the pines, spruces, and aspens that are its woodland companions. Its beauty glistens in the winter sunlight as its distinctive curls of scrolling white bark uncover a

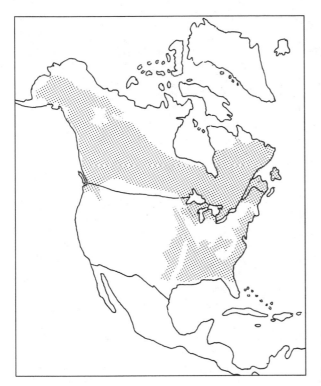

This map shows the vast area covered by the five native species of birch trees.

rich orange bark that lies beneath. Look for white birches scattered through-out the eastern woodlands in association with sugar maples, gray and yellow birches, northern red oaks, and wild black cherries. Although birches are con-sidered trees of intermediate height, the white birch can grow to a towering eighty feet. This characteristic immediately distinguishes it from its smaller cousin, the gray birch.

The gray birch has nearly nonpeeling white bark flecked with "eyebrows" at the bases of its branches. This tree reaches a height of no more than thirty-three feet, and its slender trunk rarely exceeds six inches in diameter. Its small size belies its tough nature, however. You can expect to see gray birches in overgrown, neglected pastures and in fire-scarred gravelly land, as well as along the margins of wetlands. Sandy soils also host these rugged trees.

Each autumn, gray birches shed their leaves, which decay and release much-needed nutrients into the impoverished soil. These fragile-looking trees are "nurses" for pine and hardwood seedlings that flourish in the shade provided by the foliage of the mature gray birch. Because it grows rapidly,

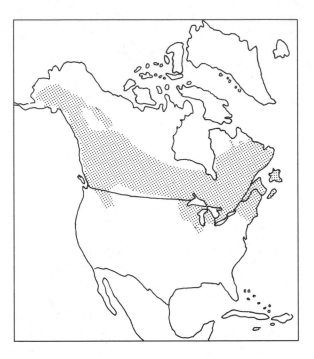

Range of the white birch
(Betula papyrifera)

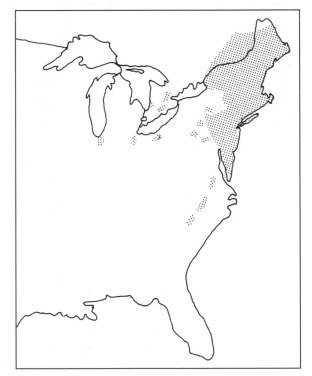

Range of the gray birch
(Betula populifolia)

THE LIFE

improves the soil, and initially grows where other trees will not, the gray birch has been dubbed a "pioneer tree."

It may come as a surprise that not all birch trees have white bark. The yellow birch (*Betula alleghaniensis*) sports a silvery bark when young but becomes a yellowish or reddish brown as it matures. It can reach a majestic height of seventy to eighty feet. Yellow birches grow in moist, cool regions in association with hemlock, balsam fir, white pine, red spruce, and hardwoods such as sugar maple, black cherry, and beech. The yellow birch was unknown until discovered in 1803 by the French botanist André Michaux. Unlike the showy white birches, these trees don't call attention to themselves, but you may notice their clear golden foliage in the autumn.

The sweet birch (*Betula lenta*) has two distinctive characteristics: black bark that doesn't peel, and the strong smell of wintergreen noticeable if you snap a small twig. Yellow birch has a hint of the aroma, but the bark of the two birches is different. The dark bark of the sweet birch resembles that of a cherry tree and gives this birch another of its common names, cherry birch. Look for the sweet birch scattered among white oak, white pine, yellow birch, basswood, hemlock, and yellow poplar.

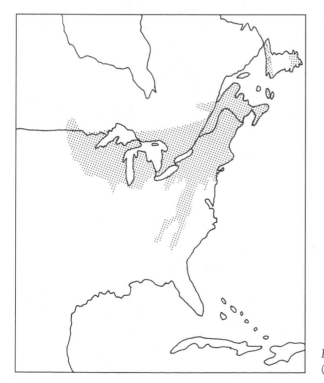

Range of the yellow birch
(Betula alleghaniensis)

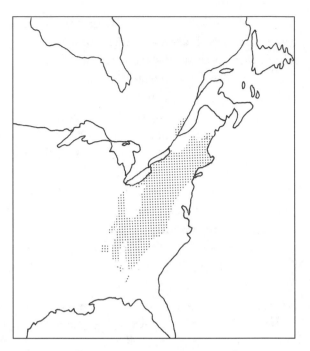

Range of the sweet birch
(Betula lenta)

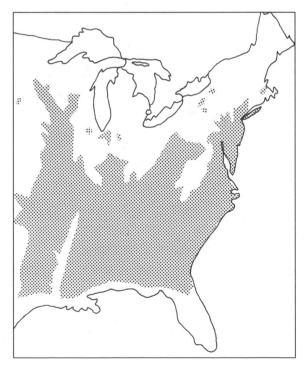

Range of the river birch
(Betula nigra)

THE LIFE

The sweet birch was once valued commercially for the oil of wintergreen it produced. Appalachian families would hunt the woodlands for young trees, which they harvested and chopped into chips. Oil of wintergreen was processed from the wood chips and sold. Unfortunately, it took one hundred trees to produce one quart of oil. Today, oil of wintergreen is manufactured synthetically from wood alcohol and salicylic acid. There is no doubt that chemists came to the rescue of the sweet birch!

The river birch (*Betula nigra*), like its cousins, is familiar with snow and freezing temperatures, even though its range extends south into Florida. Unlike its relatives, which prefer higher altitudes, the river birch, as its name implies, prefers the clay soils typically found in river valleys. Look for the dignified river birch growing along the banks of streams and rivulets that meander throughout the countryside. It can be found along the banks of sluggish rivers such as the Merrimack in Massachusetts and along the many tributaries of the Mississippi. In these lowlands, you will find sycamores, silver maples, red maples, cottonwoods, willows, and elms thriving beside the river birch.

Like most of the other birch trees, the river birch has peeling bark. On young trees, the reddish brown, paper-thin, scaly bark scrolls back to reveal a hint of pink on the brownish bark beneath. As the trees mature, they develop a coarse, dark, scalelike bark that does not fit our typical idea of birchbark.

All of these birch species are wind pollinated and produce tiny winged fruits that are scattered by the slightest breeze. Each spring, male and female flowers appear in separate clusters, known as catkins, on the same tree. The male catkins are long and pendulous; the female catkins tend to be short and stubby. You can find some catkins on the trees throughout the winter. If you find them on a twig, shake it, and you will experience a shower of winged seeds. Gray birches produce seeds when they are ten years old, paper birches when they are fifteen, but sweet and river birches don't produce seeds until they reach the ripe old age of forty.

Yellow birch has substantial commercial value. Its timber was once used in shipbuilding, but today its wood is valued for more domestic uses. The close-grained, red heartwood is used to make cutting boards and other wooden ware, as well as high-quality furniture and kitchen cabinets. The less-dense wood of white birch is a good turning wood and is used to make spindles and stair balusters. Sweet birch is used for lumber, baskets, wooden ware, and crates. Wood from sweet birch and yellow birch also makes excellent wine kegs and barrels.

Two other members of the birch family, ironwood, or American hornbeam (*Carpinus caroliniana*), and hophornbeam (*Ostrya virginiana*), sometimes also known as ironwood, are widespread throughout the eastern part of the United States. Although they are less obvious and not well known, they deserve mention as members of the family. Along with the confusion that surrounds their common names, another reason for their obscurity is that they are small and their presence fades in the company of taller trees. Hophornbeam reaches only twenty-three to forty feet in height and is hidden by the leafy greenery of sugar maples, beeches, yellow birches, and basswood. Ironwood, at thirteen to twenty-six feet, is overshadowed by bur oaks, sweet gums, and northern red oaks.

Small trees that grow beneath larger ones are called understory trees. Dogwood, redbud, and holly are three other common trees that also occupy this ecological niche. To survive in this habitat, the trees need to adapt to diminished sunlight. They have done so by developing a system of spreading branches, which you can easily see during the winter months. This adapta-

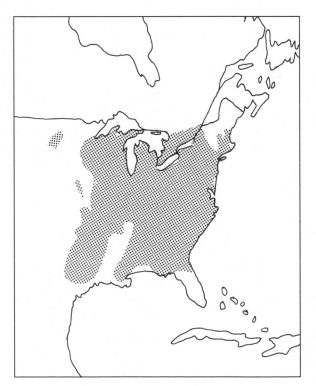

Range of ironwood
(Carpinus caroliniana)

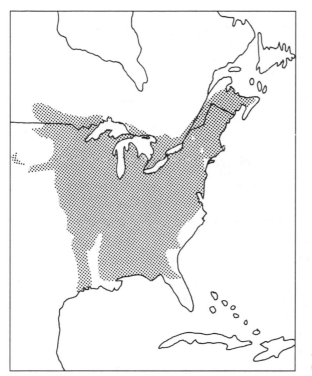

Range of the hophornbeam
(Ostrya virginiana)

tion allows the food-producing leaves to capture the dappled sunlight that filters through the canopy formed by taller trees.

When exploring the woodlands, look for the hophornbeam, which you can identify by its thin, flaky, gray bark. The smooth, fluted gray bark of ironwood resembles a human limb with flexed muscles rippling under the skin, hence another common name, musclewood. This trait results from unequal growth in the bark-producing cells.

Like other members of the birch family (Betulaceae), the hophornbeam produces catkins. Its leaves and twigs are browsed on by deer, while various songbirds, squirrels, and grouse nibble on seeds and catkins. These foods are of limited value, however, and wildlife resort to them only to fend off extreme hunger. The wood of hophornbeam makes good axe and mallet handles; otherwise, it has little commercial value.

The real value of the trees of the birch family does not lie in commerce, however. A birch tree gracing a field or pasture is truly a thing of beauty, and therein lies its value.

THE WORLD OF DECIDUOUS TREES

What you will need	Science skills
basic kit	*observing*
camera and film	*recording*
perseverance	*inferring*

OBSERVATIONS

Becoming a tree watcher is an excellent way to improve your observational skills, and a field notebook is a wonderful tool to help you organize those observations. Although you can arrange the information any way you like, it is helpful to begin by planning the book around tree types. For example, you could keep all of the information you collect about oak trees in a section apart from the information you collect about birch trees. Include seasonal observations, photographs, illustrations, wildlife interactions with the trees, and any community issues that may involve trees where you live. The notebook can be as simple or as involved as you like. This adventure could be the beginning of an enduring friendship with trees.

Which Is Which. Now that you know there are several different kinds of birch trees, you may want to begin your study of trees by learning to distinguish one birch from another. Here are some helpful hints to get you started.

1. You can always tell the paper birch *(Betula papyrifera)* by its white, tissue-thin bark that scrolls back from the trunk to reveal bright orange inner bark. This tree has several other common names, which can make things a little confusing. One nickname, canoe birch, reflects a famous use for the bark. The labels white birch and silver birch also are used to describe this tree.

2. The gray birch *(B. populifolia)* has dull gray-white bark that, in contrast with that of the white birch, hardly peels at all. You can also identify the tree by the black "eyebrows" that develop below the base of branches. Finally, the gray birch is the small birch that grows in fields, and it frequently develops in clusters of several stems that grow from one root system.

3. The bark of the yellow birch *(B. alleghaniensis)* peels in small horizontal scrolls, which, on older trees, makes them look messy. As the tree ages, the color of the bark changes from a bright silvery gray to a reddish or yellowish brown. Look for this tree among sugar maple, American beech, hemlock, red spruce, balsam fir, and white pine. Its preferred habitat is cool with moist soil.

paper birch bark

gray birch bark

yellow birch bark

4. Sweet birch (*B. lenta*) is always scattered among white pine, yellow birch, sugar maple, beech, cherry, white oak, basswood, yellow poplar, and hemlock. Its smooth, dark red to nearly black bark is marked with thin horizontal scars left by old branches. You also can see breathing pores or lenticels on the bark. Break one of the light reddish brown twigs and you will notice the distinct odor of wintergreen.

5. The range of the river birch (*B. nigra*) extends farther south than that of the other birch trees. Its light reddish bark becomes a flaky silvery gray in older trees and is a clue to their identity. It is the only birch that you will find with nonwhite bark by the riverside.

Picture the Bark. Photographing the bark of each species at different stages in its development will give you a "diary" of the trees as they age. (See Chapter Note 1 to find out how bark forms.) It may be difficult for you to find a young, middle-aged, and old tree of each birch type in your neighborhood; you may have to go on a treasure hunt as you travel with your parents or friends. Getting a complete set of pictures for each kind of birch tree can take a long time and a lot of observing on your part, but scientists must work.

A Dead Birch. Compared with other trees, birch trees grow fast and have short lives. For example, the life span of the gray birch is only fifty years, and

sweet birch bark

river birch bark

a long-lived birch is about one hundred years old when it dies, compared with the eastern white oak, for example, which lives for about three hundred years. The "Methuselah" of the birches is the yellow birch. This slow-growing tree has been known to live for two hundred years. The interiors of dead branches begin to decay very quickly, even while they are still on the tree. Soon a battalion of decay organisms has reduced the interior to mush. The trees rid themselves of these nonproductive limbs quite easily with help from the wind. What remains of such a branch, or of the trunk itself, if it has died as well, is a tube of outer bark filled with rotting wood. If you find some of this dead wood, examine it. What is the decaying material like? What color is it? Is it dry or wet? What is its texture? Can you see any insects in the mushy interior?

Male or Female? Some trees, such as holly, have either male or female flowers; it is the female holly tree that bears red berries. Each birch tree, however, has both male and female flower parts growing in separate clusters or catkins. The male catkins are long and dangle from the twigs, but the female catkins are short and stubby. Look for them along the twigs and at the tips of branches. The female catkins yield prodigious amounts of lightweight, winged seeds. Every few years, the tree produces an exceptionally large crop.

Look for the catkins during the winter. Do you find more male or more female catkins at this time of the year? Keep track of their development throughout the year. When do they form? Where on the twig do the male and female catkins develop?

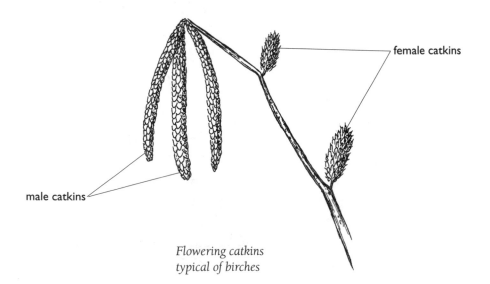

female catkins

male catkins

Flowering catkins
typical of birches

Shake a branch that holds female catkins and watch the seeds pepper the snow. Put some in a sandwich bag to examine with a hand lens when you get home.

Food for Wildlife. Birch trees don't supply a great deal of food for wildlife through the winter months. However, when it is bitter cold and other food sources are not available, the food from birch trees may keep some animals from starving. Look for birds or mammals feeding on birch trees in your area. Make a chart similar to the one below to record your observations. You may see evidence of deer browsing by carefully examining the ends of twigs to see if they have been bitten off. Deer will also remove pieces of bark. Beavers will eat the inner bark of birch trees if poplar trees are not available. You will probably see bird tracks in seed-covered snow. Enlist the help of your friends. They may see some things that you miss.

BIRCH AS A FOOD SOURCE FOR WILDLIFE

Tree Type	Animal	Part of Tree Eaten
Gray birch	Grouse and squirrels	Flower clusters and buds
	Songbirds and smaller rodents	Tiny seeds
White birch	Moose and deer	Twigs
	Grouse	Buds
	Small rodents and birds	Tiny seeds
Sweet birch	Grouse	Catkins, buds, and seeds
	Songbirds	Seeds
	White-tailed deer, beavers, moose, and porcupines	Twigs and young leaves
Yellow birch	Grouse, white-tailed deer, moose, cottontail rabbits, red squirrels	Seeds and twigs
River birch	White-tailed deer	Young twigs and buds
	Grouse, turkeys, small birds, and rodents	Tiny seeds

BRANCHING OUT FROM BIRCHES

Most people identify trees by their leaves. This makes tree identification a special challenge in winter. This may not be a disadvantage, because it forces you to observe the more subtle differences among trees.

Branch Patterns. Deciduous trees are those that shed their leaves in the fall. Without their leaves, you can see the trees' various shapes. This is an ideal time to learn about branching patterns. The diagrams will help you determine which pattern each tree illustrates.

1. Whorled branches grow out of the trunk in threes. This occurs rarely, but you can find it easily in larches (pine family), a deciduous gymnosperm.

2. The branches, twigs, and leaves are paired in some trees. Look for this pattern, called opposite, in maple, buckeye, ash, dogwood, and horse chestnut.

3. The third pattern of branch arrangement is called alternate. The branches and twigs grow in spiral steps.

If you would like to learn more about patterns in nature, read *Fascinating Fibonaccis,* by Trudi Garland (see the Bibliography).

Tree Shape. Within the parameters of a tree's genetic code, its shape is determined by its environment. A tree growing in an open space will develop a different shape than will a tree of the same type growing in more cramped quarters such as woods or an urban park. A tree that grows close to its neighbors will have normal-sized limbs only near its top, with perhaps a few

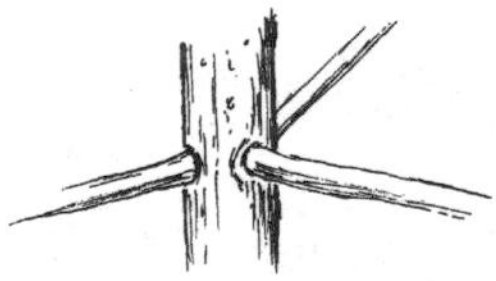

whorled
(third branch on
the other side)

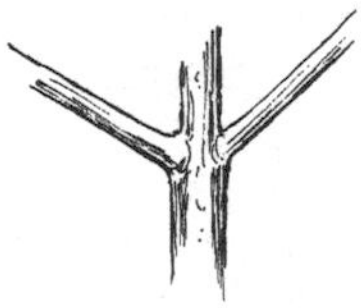

*Branching as
seen in winter*

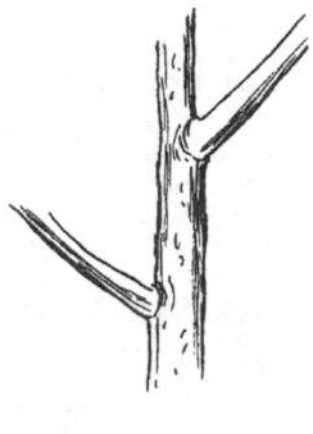

opposite, or paired

alternate

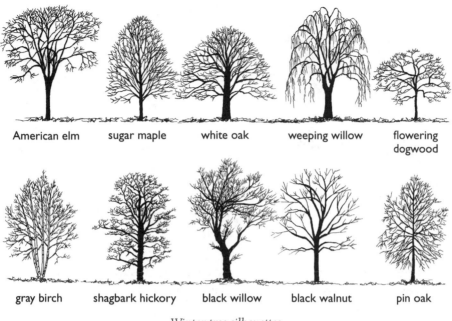

| American elm | sugar maple | white oak | weeping willow | flowering dogwood |

| gray birch | shagbark hickory | black willow | black walnut | pin oak |

Winter tree silhouettes

underdeveloped limbs along the length of its trunk. Look for this kind of stunted development.

The shape of a tree aids in its identification. For example, a sugar maple is shaped like an egg standing on its broad end. An elm looks like an open umbrella or an upside-down bud vase. To see the distinct shape of a tree, you will need to observe the tree from a distance. You can easily do this in an open field or on a golf course.

Find a tree that interests you. Describe its shape in your notebook. Draw an outline of the tree or photograph it. Do the branches droop like those of a weeping willow? Do they spread out from the trunk like a white oak, or do they grow close to the trunk like a hickory? Are the branches growing in any particular direction? Besides the prevailing winds, what might cause the tree to grow in a particular direction?

Identifying Trees by Their Bark. It is difficult to determine the identity of many trees by examining only the bark. One reason for this is that as a tree ages, its bark changes. Nevertheless, there are some trees that have very distinctive bark and are easily recognizable throughout their lives.

The sycamore (*Platanus occidentalis*) is easily identified by its mottled and flaking bark. It is frequently planted as a shade tree, and you can find it in parks and along urban and suburban streets.

American
beech bark
(Fagus grandifolia)

shagbark
hickory bark
(Carya ovata)

American
hornbeam bark
(Carpinus caroliniana)

sycamore bark
(Platanus occidentalis)

A clue to the nature of the bark of shagbark hickory (*Carya ovata*) lies in the tree's name. Strips of bark scroll away from the trunk and give the tree a shaggy appearance.

The bark of the American beech (*Fagus grandifolia*) is smooth and gray or blue-gray.

The bark of the American hornbeam (*Carpinus caroliniana*) is often described as resembling flexed arm muscles.

Clues from Twigs. Twigs come in a variety of colors, shapes, and sizes. Make a collection starting with beech, oak, shagbark hickory, and maple, if you can find them. How many colors are there among your twigs? Are they straight, zigzag, or curved? Study the additional twig traits described below. The illustrations will help you match twig with tree.

First look at the buds. The bud at the tip of the twig is called the *terminal bud.* As it develops, it adds length to the twig. The buds that grow along the side of the twig are called *lateral buds.* They produce flowers, leaves, or new branches. Each bud is covered by overlapping scales that protect the developing tissue.

The characteristics of the terminal bud can help you identify the tree. Is the bud single or in a cluster? Is it large or small? Pointed or rounded? Hairy? Sticky? What color is it? Oak twigs have clusters of three or four terminal buds protected by brown or reddish brown scales. Beech tree twigs have only one terminal bud. Like the lateral buds, it is shiny tan and cigar shaped. Red maple twigs have a single round, dark red terminal bud. The terminal bud of shagbark hickory is elongated with blunt tips, hairy, and usually dark brown.

Now look at the lateral buds along the sides of the twigs. How do they resemble the terminal buds?

The small dots you see on new or young twigs are *lenticels*. These are openings in the outer layers of the stem and root tissues that allow the exchange of oxygen into and carbon dioxide out of the plant. Is there a pattern to the arrangement of lenticels? How far back on the twig can you find them?

Twigs will also show *leaf scars*. During the summer, the tree produces a layer of cork between the leaf stem and the point where it attaches to the twig. When this layer is complete, the leaf falls, and the mark left on the twig is called the leaf scar. The shape of the leaf scar is unique for each type of tree. If you look closely at a bare twig, you will see tiny dots in the leaf scar. These dots mark where the transport tubes of the twig joined those of the leaf and are called the vascular bundle scar. The illustrations below show lateral buds and leaf scars on selected twigs. You will notice that they come in a variety of shapes and sizes. The color of the buds also will vary according to the type of tree.

The *terminal bud scar* is the point where the bud scales of the terminal bud were attached. The space between rings, which look like rubber bands

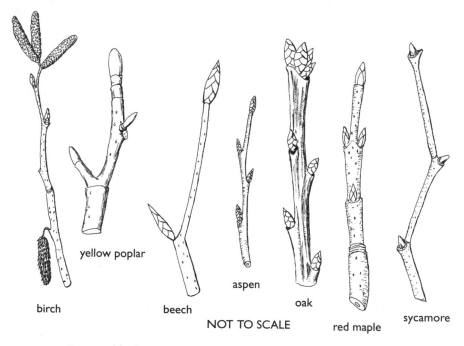

birch   yellow poplar   beech   aspen   oak   red maple   sycamore

NOT TO SCALE

Twigs and buds are especially useful in identifying trees in winter.

around the twig, mark each year's growth. In what year did your twig grow the most? Look at other twigs the same age on the same tree. Do they also show the most growth during that same year?

If you cut into a twig, you will find a spongelike substance called *pith*. When placed in a growth medium, pieces of pith grow into new plants. Cut a cross section of twig and examine the pith. If it is star-shaped, it is probably an oak, poplar, or hickory twig. If the pith is circular, it is probably an elm twig.

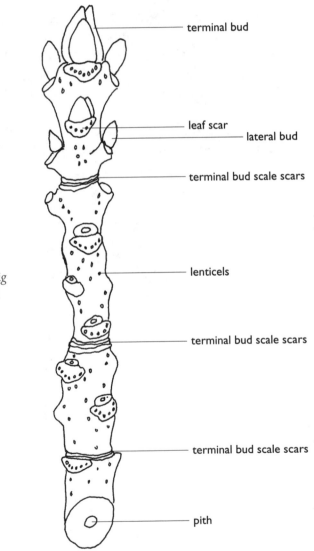

Green ash twig with terminal bud.

THE LIFE

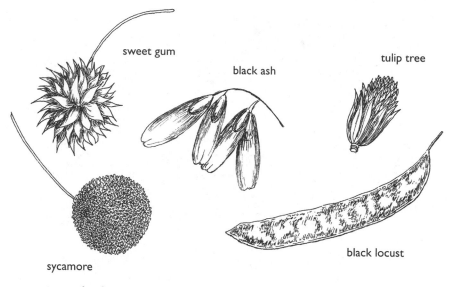

sweet gum

black ash

tulip tree

sycamore

black locust

Many deciduous trees retain some seed containers throughout the winter.

Seed Containers. Many deciduous trees retain some seed containers throughout the winter. You can easily see the button balls, or seed clusters, of the sycamore dangling from the zigzag twigs. If you live in an area where sweet gum (*Liquidambar styraciflua*) thrive, look for the spiked seed balls. Clusters of winged seeds that hang from branches announce the ash. The yellow poplar or tulip tree (*Liriodendron tulipifera*) produces seed clusters that resemble a tulip blossom. Ash trees (*Fraxinus* spp.) retain bunches of winged seeds. See if you can find these and other trees that retain some seed containers throughout the winter.

CHAPTER NOTES

1. A tree grows in length and in width. It grows in length both at the tips of the roots and in the buds at the tips of twigs and branches. In these places, delicate developing tissue called meristem is found. When triggered by hormones, the meristem develops and causes the twigs and roots to grow longer.

Trees also grow in circumference. Cambium, the thin tissue responsible for this growth, lies beneath the bark. This tissue is only two or three cells thick. The cambium layer covers the entire tree, from the smallest rootlets to the most delicate branches. Through the action of the cambium, all parts of the tree become thicker.

Toward the end of winter, longer and longer periods of daylight trigger the manufacture of growth hormones, such as auxin and gibberellin, by

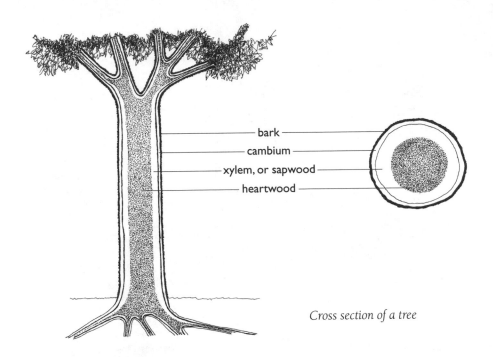

bark
cambium
xylem, or sapwood
heartwood

Cross section of a tree

embryonic tissue. This underdeveloped tissue is located in the leaf buds at the ends of twigs and branches. The growth chemicals cause developing cells to grow and divide, adding length to the branches and height to the tree. At the root ends, a similar process results in longer roots.

At about the same time, the growth hormones produced in the twigs and branches acivate the girth-producing cambium. The cells of the cambium sheath grow vigorously toward the outside of the tree. After several weeks, these cells mature and cease dividing. Stiffened with cellulose, these older cells become specialized into hollow, food-carrying tubes called phloem. The phloem system transports carbohydrates manufactured in the green leaves to the branches, trunk, and roots. As the phloem cells age, new cells replace them and push them toward the outside of the tree. The old cells eventually become part of the outer bark. With the help of a hand lens, you can sometimes see the living phloem in a freshly cut log as a circle of black dots just inside the outer bark.

Each tree species is programmed to form patterns that make plates, fissures, and cracks that distinguish it from all other species.

CHAPTER 5

Cedars

WINTER GREEN

If you go out into the woods or a park in the winter almost anywhere in North America, you notice that some trees remain green and others are leafless skeletons. By making this observation, you have divided the trees into two groups: those trees that lose their leaves, known as deciduous trees, and those that remain green throughout the year, called evergreens.

Scientists also separate trees into two groups by another set of criteria. Some trees have seeds enclosed in a container, such as apple, oak, and maple. Other trees, such as pine, spruce, hemlock, and cedar, have naked seeds that lie exposed on the "shelves" of cones.

The container seed trees are called angiosperms and the naked seed trees gymnosperms. This classification is very useful, because some deciduous trees, such as the larch, are gymnosperms.

The angiosperms are relatively recent arrivals on the earth. They are part of a large group of plant life that evolved during the Cretaceous period about 100 million years ago, the flowering plants. Gymnosperms have been around much longer. Their origin dates back to the Carboniferous period, some 350 million years ago. These ancient plants were part of the diet of plant-eating dinosaurs.

Today one of the most widespread conifers, or cone-bearing trees, east of the Mississippi is the eastern red cedar. This tree is not as familiar to most people as the members of the pine (Pinaceae) family used to decorate our homes for Christmas. The yellow-green spires of eastern red cedars are also part of the winter landscape, but they get only superficial attention. They are generally looked upon as prickly weed trees that grow in waste places, and it frequently comes as a surprise that they, like pines and spruce, are also cone-bearing trees.

Although we refer to the trees as cedars, botanists tell us that there are no true cedars (*Cedrus* spp.) growing wild in the United States. Cedars grow naturally in North African countries, the Himalayas, and Southeast Asia. Although you may see deodar or Lebanon cedars as landscape plantings in a neighbor's yard, they are not native trees. Our field tree is actually a juniper and is properly called *Juniperus virginiana*. It is a member of the cedar or cypress family (Cupressaceae) and a close cousin to the arborvitaes and cypresses.

Even if you forget the formal nomenclature, you will probably not forget the delicate veil of blue berries, each with a white wash, that covers the cedars each autumn. The berrylike fruits scattered throughout the foliage are actually cones with a fleshy covering. Early in their development they are green, but at maturity they become blue with a waxy gray coat. Perhaps it is fitting that the cedar tree that is not a cedar should have berries that are not berries. Since these cones look like berries, get eaten like berries, and contain seeds like berries, let's continue to call them berries for our purposes.

The berries (cones) supply wildlife with nourishment during the cold season. Although a single berry is not very nutritious, each tree makes up for this deficiency by producing a prodigious number of them. One dedicated investigator counted more than a million berries on one tree. You may have seen clouds of birds such as cedar waxwings and robins crowding the trees during the fall migration. When more nutritious fare is not available throughout the winter, the berries nourish as many as sixty-three species of birds. One cedar waxwing was observed eating fifty-three berries in one hour. People who have eastern red cedars on their property or live near abandoned fields that support these trees tell us it takes only a few days for flocks of yellow-rumped warblers, robins, and starlings to strip eastern red cedars of their berries. Gamebirds are also good customers at the Red Cedar Café. Quail, pheasant, turkeys, and grouse are among the regular guests that dine there.

Small animals such as deer mice also find nourishment in the berries throughout the cold weather. This is convenient because the trees also offer housing. The little mice retreat into abandoned birds' nests, which they line with soft plant material to insulate and add comfort throughout the winter months.

When eaten, the seeds within the berries pass through the digestive tracts of the foraging animals. Scientists believe this is an advantage to the trees because the process improves the germination rate of the seeds. Many roadside red cedars have been inadvertently planted by birds resting on overhead telephone wires. The next time you see a row of eastern red cedars along the roadside, thank our friends the birds. Mice living in fields and thickets also eat the berries and disperse the seeds in their droppings along their runways, in this way scattering eastern red cedars across fields.

Eastern red cedar trees are either male or female. Female trees are easily recognized by the crop of blue berries they produce each year. Although male trees may produce some berries, they are better known for the tiny, cylindrical, yellow cones that develop at the tips of branchlets. Each year female trees yield berries, but every three years they produce an extra large crop of seeds. The seeds may take as long as three years to germinate.

The foliage of eastern red cedars is a warm yellow-green with a hint of brown or bronze. Although red cedars don't shed their needles each autumn, the needles are not a permanent part of the tree. They grow old, turn brown,

new foliage

old foliage

eastern red cedar (Juniperus virginiana)

fall, and are replaced by new growth. Because only a small percentage of the needles do this at one time, the tree is never bare. Even old and dead foliage remains on the trees for several years after its ability to manufacture food has ceased. This old foliage is responsible for the trees' brownish hue. Many conifers in the pine family, such as pine, hemlock, fir, and spruce, share this trait.

Throughout the tree, the leaves, or needles, of eastern red cedars are not uniformly shaped. Foliage on red cedars is quite different from that of the pines, whose needles are wrapped with tan papery sheaths into neat bundles of two, three, or five. The new growth near the tips of the branches is lance shaped and prickly, but older foliage consists of overlapping, thick, blunt scales that cover four-sided twigs and branches. In the activities that follow, you will have an opportunity to observe the differences between the foliage of eastern red cedars and members of the pine family.

Red cedars live equally well in moist, swampy areas and in dry, poorly nourished soils. Among the eastern conifers such as eastern white pines (*Pinus strobus*) and eastern hemlocks (*Tsuga canadensis*), eastern red cedars are blue-ribbon winners in their ability to thrive in droughty areas. Although they are generally seen growing alone in abandoned fields, you may also see them in loosely formed groves. Red cedars are trees of open, sun-drenched fields, but it is not unusual to find them growing among loosely spaced hickories, oaks, and shortleaf pines.

They are important trees in field ecology. Although they can withstand a wide range of soil acidity, they are often found growing in alkaline soils. The decomposition of their litter tends to make acidic soil more alkaline. Scientists have found that where eastern red cedars grow, the soil favors earthworm activity.

Eastern red cedars were nearly totally destroyed through the manufacture of pencils, cedar-lined closets, and chests. Poor planning and at least a dollop of greed were responsible for this near disaster. Insence-cedar (*Libocedrus decurrens*) from the West Coast is used for aromatic lumber in place of the now scarce red cedar.

Northern white cedar (*Thuja occidentalis*), another member of the cypress or cedar family, closely resembles eastern red cedar, and the two are often mistaken for one another. They are both spiral-shaped coniferous evergreens that have scalelike leaves on their branches. The northern white cedar has a few traits that differ significantly from those of the eastern red cedar, however. Northern white cedar is an arborvitae. Unlike the solitary red cedar of abandoned fields, arborvitae grows in dense stands in moist, swampy areas and is a companion to other cone-bearing trees in the coniferous forests of the North.

The foliage of the northern white cedar, made up of small, thick, overlapping scales, completely covers the fan-shaped branchlets. If you crush the tiny spadelike leaves, you will produce an odor similar to the smoky smell that emanates from crumbled yarrow, a roadside and meadow wildflower.

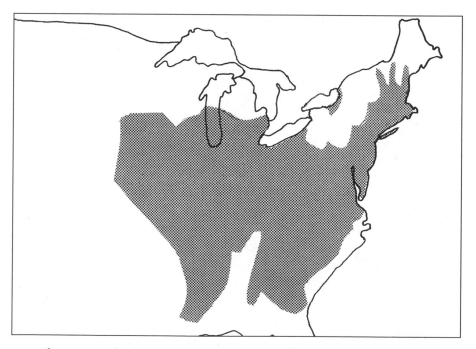

The eastern red cedar is the most widespread conifer of eastern North America.

Although these trees are not as helpful to wildlife as the eastern red cedars, they benefit some birds and animals. Finches such as pine siskins eat the tiny winged seeds produced in the cones. Red squirrels find the long wisps of peeling bark to their liking. In the spring, these squirrels feast on the trees' tender buds, and in the autumn, they harvest the small cone-laden twigs for their winter stores. In cold weather, white-tailed deer and snowshoe hares browse the northern white cedars but generally don't cause permanent damage to the trees. However, porcupines that eat the bark of the trees have been known to strip them of a circle of bark that includes the living tissue (cambium layer) that lies just beneath the dead outer bark. Although this activity benefits the porcupines, it is generally lethal for the trees.

The arborvitae, which means "tree of life," has been known to live as long as three hundred years. The reasons for the tree's longevity have been the subject of a great deal of speculation. Most trees that are long-lived have strong, hard wood, but the wood of the arborvitae is soft, weak, and brittle. Some scientists think the tree's long life may be due to resin in its wood, but there are short-lived pines that also have resin in their wood. Other scientists point to the tree's freedom from insect and fungal pests as an explanation for a long life. Fire-resistant bark and the tree's preference for moist, swampy habitats, which further protect the trees from fire damage, also have been suggested as possible clues to its longevity. But the more scientists probe, the more questions emerge.

northern white cedar
(Thuja occidentalis)

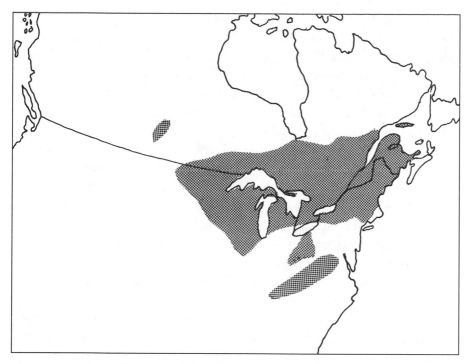

The northern white cedar, a tree of the colder regions, occurs throughout central and east-ern Canada and northern portions of the United States. It is also scattered along higher elevations of the Appalachian Mountains.

Thousands of years ago, when *Thuja occidentalis* first appeared on earth, instructions for long-term survival were spelled out in the tree's genetic code. Only the trees know that message, and perhaps someday they will share it with us.

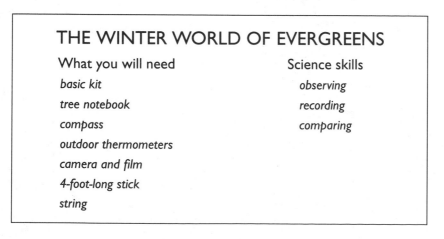

THE WINTER WORLD OF EVERGREENS

What you will need	Science skills
basic kit	*observing*
tree notebook	*recording*
compass	*comparing*
outdoor thermometers	
camera and film	
4-foot-long stick	
string	

OBSERVATIONS

Cedars, along with other cone-bearing trees, are gymnosperms. Gymnosperms produce seeds, but unlike the angiosperms (flowering plants), their seeds are not enclosed within a fruit such as an apple or an acorn. The seeds of gymnosperms are naked. They develop on the tiny "shelves" that make up the woody female cones we associate with hemlocks, pines, cedars, spruces, and other coniferous evergreen trees.

The most familiar gymnosperms are the cone-bearing trees (conifers). The largest number of conifers belong to the pine family (Pinaceae), which includes pines, spruces, hemlocks, larches, Douglas firs, and true firs. The cedar or cypress family (Cupressaceae) includes other cone-bearing trees, such as cedars and junipers.

The Deciduous Conifer. The terms *evergreen* and *conifer* should not be used synonymously, because there are cone-bearing trees that lose their leaves. The American larch, or tamarack *(Larix laricina),* and the imported European, or common, larch *(Larix decidua)* are examples of deciduous conifers.

These trees produce cones yet shed their needlelike leaves each autumn after an exquisite fiery orange display that rivals the most flamboyant deciduous tree. You may see a larch during the fall season that becomes a more subdued yellow-orange. In either case, the larch contributes handsomely to

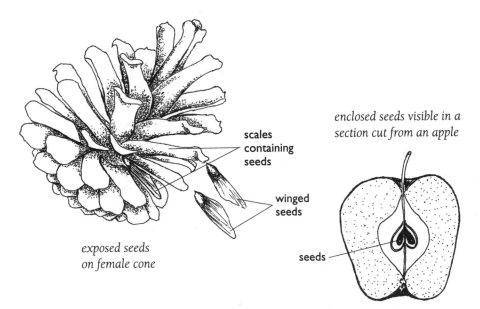

scales
containing
seeds

winged
seeds

*exposed seeds
on female cone*

*enclosed seeds visible in a
section cut from an apple*

seeds

A comparison between gymnosperm seeds and enclosed angiosperm seeds

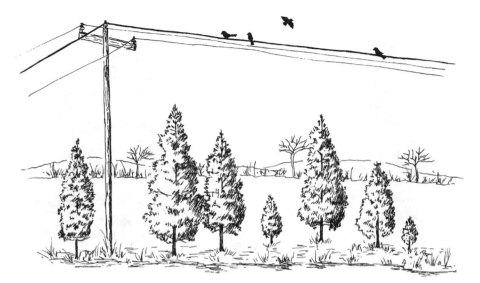

Look for eastern red cedars along the road or beneath telephone wire.

the fall show of color. The common larch has been widely planted in the northern part of the United States and in Canada, where it thrives along with our native species.

Larches may be difficult to find in your area. Ask at a local nature center or nursery where larches grow near your home. Observe them. Record the dates of your observations and write descriptions of what happens. Does the tree change color all at once, or is it a gradual change that occurs over a period of a few weeks or several weeks?

Neighborhood Excursion. Eastern red cedars are typically among the first trees to invade an abandoned field. Look for the floppy yellow-green branchlets atop the spire shape of maturing trees scattered throughout a field. How many eastern red cedars are there in the field? Are the trees growing in tight clusters or are they some distance from one another? Can you identify a pattern of trees in a field that might indicate the location of a runway made by deer mice? Other places to look for eastern red cedars are along the side of the road or beneath telephone wires. Birds resting on the overhead wires frequently deposit in their fecal material seeds from the cedar cones they ate. Also look for cedars at the edge of a wood lot or forested area.

Record the location of any tree you find in your special tree notebook, along with drawings, photographs, and comments. Describe the tree. What is its shape? Young eastern red cedars resemble church spires. A close examination of the growth pattern of the branches will explain this shape. The

eastern red cedar
(Juniperus virginiana)

eastern white pine
(Pinus strobus)

Eastern red cedar branches grow upward, hugging the tree trunk.

branches seem to hug the tree trunk as they grow upward. Compare this with the branching pattern of an eastern white pine *(Pinus·strobus)*.

What color is the foliage? Observe the tree throughout the year. How does its color change from season to season? Where is the dead foliage located? Compare this with the dead foliage on a pine tree.

Look for berries and cones. Is the tree a male or female? Where on the branches are the berries or cones located? At the tips or along the length of the branches? When do they appear?

Funny Foliage. The coniferous evergreens that are most familiar to us produce leaves, or needles, that are more or less uniform throughout the tree. For example, the needles on an eastern white pine grow along the tree's twigs and branches in bundles that each contain five needles that are from three to five inches long. The stiff, often sharp leaves of spruce grow singly, are stalkless, and sit directly on the twigs.

In contrast, the foliage of the eastern red cedar is not uniform throughout the tree. Compare the foliage at the tip of a branch with the foliage an inch or so back on the twig. How far from the tip does the twig become woody? Is the twig round, square, or triangular? A hand lens will give you a better view of the twig and the foliage. Write a description of the foliage so that a friend could distinguish eastern red cedars from members of the pine family such as eastern white pine (*Pinus strobus*) or spruce (*Picea* spp.). The foliage on white pine and spruce extends along the branches toward the trunk, but is this the case with eastern red cedar?

Compare the foliage of the eastern red cedar with that of a northern white cedar or arborvitae (*Thuja occidentalis*). If you don't live within the natural range of these trees, you may have a neighbor who has landscaped a yard with some of them. Ask permission to examine those trees.

How is the foliage from the eastern red cedar similar to that of the northern white cedar and how is it different? Make drawings of some foliage from these two trees. Include the drawings in your notebook under the coniferous evergreens section. If you cannot draw, photographs are an excellent way to capture detail.

A secret of success for cedars and other winter evergreens lies in the toughness of their needles, which protect the more delicate structures that lie beneath the surface. You can feel the protective waxy coat. If you were to figure out the total surface area of the needles, you would be amazed at the area devoted to photosynthesis.

Bark. The characteristics of outer bark are unique to each tree species. One of the properties of cedar bark is its odor. You can smell the beautiful aroma if you sniff close to a section of peeling bark. Cedar bark peels in a unique way. Look for the upward curling strips that characterize this group of trees. Note that the eastern red cedar is a member of the cypress family, not the pine family. For a discussion of tree bark, see Chapter Note 1 in the previous chapter.

PINE FAMILY MEMBERS

The pine family is a very large group of conifers, most of whose members are familiar Christmas tree species. In the activities that follow, you will have a chance to look at many of these trees. Winter is a good time to begin making observations, when pines stand out among the skeletons of deciduous trees.

Key Pine Family Traits. Each of the many types of evergreens has special characteristics that distinguish it from others. Several groups of pines are found throughout North America. To which groups do your trees belong?

Pine (*Pinus* spp.). The only cone-bearing evergreens that actually have needle-shaped leaves. Make a cross section of a pine needle and examine the cut with a magnifier. If the needle is from a soft pine, you will see only one vein. If it is from a hard pine, you will see two veins.

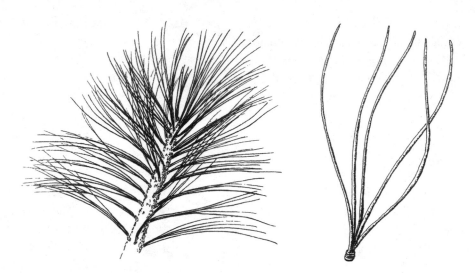

The soft bluish green needles of the eastern white pine (Pinus strobus) *are three to five inches long and grow in bundles of five held togehter by a tan wrap or sheath.*

Spruce (*Picea* spp.). The tree is shaped like a pyramid. The needles have sharp points, grow separately on the twig, and stick out in all directions, so the twig does not lie flat. Needles are four-sided, grow on short pegs, and leave rough spots where they have fallen off.

Hemlock (*Tsuga* spp.). These trees have a feathery appearance and characteristic nodding topknot. The needles of the eastern hemlock are dark green

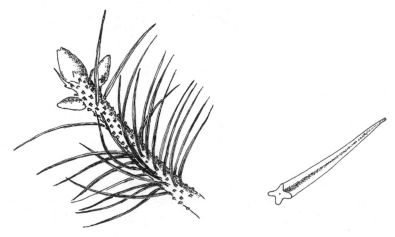

The four-sided needles of spruce (Picea spp.) *grow singly on short projections, or pegs. When the needles fall off the twig, these pegs make the twig rough to the touch. In enlarged cross section, the four-sided design of an individual needle is apparent.*

and flat. They grow in one plane, so the twigs lie flat. Look for white lines on the undersurface of the needles. These are caused by closely packed breathing pores, or stomates.

True fir (*Abies* spp.). The bark is smooth with resin blisters. The needles occur singly, tend to curve upward, and look as though they grow out of the top of twigs. If you remove one, you will see a round scar. Cones sit upright.

Larch (*Larix* spp.). This pyramid-shaped tree is the only member of the pine family that sheds its needles each fall. The soft needles are apple green and grow in tufts on stubby twigs. Look for the knobs that cover twigs and branches.

Douglas fir (*Pseudotsuga menziesii*). This member of the family is found growing naturally only west of the Rocky Mountains. Cones occur on both upper and lower branches. A three-pronged bract protrudes from behind every scale.

Variations in the Pine Family. Find a few different members of the pine family. What is the shape of each? Is it triangular (conical)? Does the tree look stiff and rigid or light and feathery? Is it blue-green, yellow-green, or some other shade of green?

Look at the needles on the twigs. How are they arranged? Are they in little bundles? How many needles are in each bundle? Is there a tan wrap around the base of each bundle? Roll one of the needles between your fingers. Is it round or angular? Cut across the needle and examine its shape with a hand lens.

| Norway spruce | eastern white pine | eastern hemlock |
| (*Picea abies*) | (*Pinus strobus*) | (*Tsuga canadensis*) |

Trees of the pine family are easy to identify by their typical Christmas-tree shape.

In some members of the pine family, such as spruce and hemlock, the needles grow singly on the twigs rather than in bundles. Are the needles attached to the twigs by little stems?

A Cone Collection. When we talk of evergreen cones, we are usually talking about the more conspicuous female, or seed-bearing, cones. These cones are as varied as the trees that produce them.

Where on the tree do you find them? At the top third of the tree? The top half? Are they at the ends of the twigs? Carefully examine cones from different trees. Are they soft and pliable or hard and rigid? Do they have prickles? Are they curved or straight? How long are they? How wide? How are the cones attached to the twig? Is there a stalk? Are the cones growing opposite each other on the twig?

Examine the scales from a cone. Do you see scars or slight depressions in

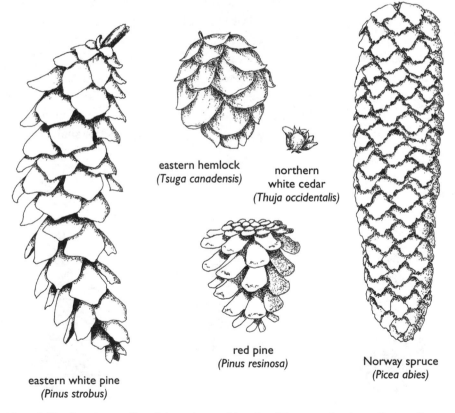

eastern hemlock
(*Tsuga canadensis*)

northern
white cedar
(*Thuja occidentalis*)

red pine
(*Pinus resinosa*)

Norway spruce
(*Picea abies*)

eastern white pine
(*Pinus strobus*)

The soft bluish green needles of the eastern white pine (Pinus strobus) *are three to five inches long and grow in bundles of five held togehter by a tan wrap or sheath.*

THE LIFE

the scales? How many depressions are there on each scale? Are there any seeds in your cones?

When you have collected cones from a variety of different trees, select one and write a description of it. Give your description to a friend. Can your friend select the same cone from your collection without further help from you?

Examining Tree Bark. When people draw trees, they almost always color the bark brown. How accurate is this common perception?

To improve your color observations, go to the paint section of a hardware store and select some color strips you think might match the trunks of cone-bearing trees. Include browns, tans, rusts, grays, and black.

With color strips and notebook in hand, visit some evergreens and compare the colors with the tree trunks. Record your observations by cutting the matching colors from the paint charts and securing them in your notebook along with other information about the trees.

Photograph the bark at different times of day to record how shifting angles of sunlight affect color. Caption each photograph with the name of the species, its location, the date and time, and the side of the trunk you photographed (north, south, east, or west). The age of your tree can be determined by counting the number of whorls. These will be evidenced by branches that circle the trunk like the spokes around the hub of a wagon wheel. Generally there are three branches in a whorl. Don't forget to count the whorls that may have dropped from the tree. These will be evidenced by branch scars on the trunk.

Examine some twigs. Is the bark at the tip of the twig the same as the bark farther back? Look at the bark on a branch. How does it differ from the bark on the twig?

Evergreens can be identified by the patterns of plates, cracks, ridges, and fissures in the bark. The size and shape of plates in the bark change as the tree ages and expands in girth. Examine the bark on the trunks of your trees. Are the cracks vertical or horizontal? Are they slanted? How wide are they? What size and shape are the plates? Examine the bark on younger trees and compare it with the bark of older trees.

EXPLORATIONS

Tree Community. Winter is a wonderful time to learn about animals and birds that find shelter in coniferous evergreens. Look for throngs of birds such as chickadees, titmice, blue jays, cardinals, juncos, grosbeaks, and sparrows and for mammals such as raccoons and red and gray squirrels. Do the trees shelter more birds and animals at a particular time of the day?

Keep a record for a week or two. Do the birds gather in the trees at any particular time? If birds are in eastern red cedars, are they eating the berries? Which birds do this? Look for red squirrels feeding on pine cones.

EASTERN RED CEDAR COMMUNITY

Date	Time	Visitors	Activity

Evergreens as Windbreaks. How much protection against wind and weather do evergreens provide? You can find this out for yourself on any cold, windy winter day. Plan to do this investigation for several days during a stretch of cold, stormy weather. Listen to the weather forecast for your area to determine when such weather will occur. Begin by visiting a dense grove of conifers. Try standing on various sides of the trees. What differences did you notice? Did you notice any difference in the intensity and in the sound of the wind?

Find out whether a grove of evergreen trees affects temperature. Record the temperature at the middle of the grove, while surrounded by evergreens, and compare it with the temperature out in the open some distance away from the trees.

Do individual trees provide shelter from cold and wind? To find out, you will need two outdoor thermometers, a stick about four feet long, and some string. Put one end of the stick in the ground, and secure one thermometer near the top of the stick. Secure a second thermometer to the main trunk of a cedar tree at the same height above the ground as the thermometer on the stick. What do the two thermometers read? Check them at regular intervals and continue to do so as long into the night as you can. What happens? Put your information on a graph. How do the temperatures compare? Explain your findings.

Try this investigation with several other kinds of conifers such as spruce, hemlock, and pine. How do these trees rank against the eastern red cedars as wind protectors?

Freeze Resistance of Buds. Conifers can withstand very cold temperatures. The following is a partial list of trees and the lowest temperatures they can survive.

Tree	Lowest Temperature
Eastern red cedar	-112°F.
White spruce	-112°F.
Lodgepole pine	-112°F.
Northern white cedar	-112°F.
Larch	-112°F.
Live oak	18°F.

These temperatures are the lowest at which the buds on those trees will survive. Survival is also dependent, however, on the rate at which the temperature drops. Sudden cold snaps change the picture considerably, because buds do not have time to prepare for the onslaught of cold. Sudden and unseasonal rises in temperature also sap the trees' strength and cause death. Sometimes during the winter the temperature will rise to a point where the buds open. These sudden warm periods are usually followed by a cold snap, then a return to seasonal temperatures. When this happens, the open buds die.

CHAPTER 6

Winter Weeds

WILDLY SUCCESSFUL PLANTS

A sunny, bitterly cold January morning reveals a quiet world locked in a transparent case of ice. Millions of tiny lights created by the sun's rays dance on crystalline surfaces. Ice-coated tree branches glisten in the morning light. Dried flower stalks that poke above the fresh cover of snow wear a sheath of ice. In their transparent prison, the plants' delicate seedpods and stalks in subtle tones of tans, browns, and grays add a special beauty to the frigid snowscape.

The ragged stems we see are silent remnants of the boisterous weeds and wildflowers whose colors enlivened meadows and roadsides throughout the warmer months. Many of the withered stalks display the intricate framework that supported flower parts; others are simply unadorned sticks.

These stalks and sticks are called winter weeds. They are the remains of plant parts that lived above the ground during the growing season. Although they appear dead, for many of them life goes on below the ground, where strong roots continue to live even in the coldest places. In others, life continues in the form of seeds that wait for the warm rains of spring.

Winter weeds are often hardy survivors whose tenacity and perseverance enable them to take root and flourish in sun-drenched waste places where the soil is deficient in nutrients. They endure in harsh habitats where other plants cannot survive.

Success in the natural world generally refers to the ability of a living thing to reproduce. Using this criterion, no one will argue that weeds are very successful. These vigorous and opportunistic plants have an array of adaptive techniques that contribute to their reproductive success. One of their strategies for survival is the production of huge numbers of seeds, and the number manufactured by some plants is phenomenal. An industrious scientist counted 196,405 seeds in one pigweed (*Amaranthus retroflexus*) plant growing in central New York. Another tallied 511,208 seeds in a single tumblemustard (*Sisymbrium altissimum*) from the same region. Every seed contains an embryo and a supply of food wrapped in a protective covering, or seed coat, and has the potential of becoming next summer's seed-producing machine.

A bountiful supply of seeds, however, is no good without effective methods of scattering them. The seeds of thistles, dogbanes, and milkweeds are equipped with lightweight silken threads. The slightest breeze can lift the seeds from the parent plant and carry them away to places where they might germinate. Other seeds are so light that they also are widely scattered by the wind. Many seeds have membranous wings, which also are suitable for transport in light winds. Although the wind does a good job at seed dispersal, it is fickle and its strength is highly unpredictable. The wind may not blow with sufficient force when the seeds are ripe and ready for takeoff.

Animals provide another effective means for scattering seeds. Unlike the fickle wind, their movements are more predictable. Migratory birds are important movers of seeds because their migrations often coincide with the ripening of fruit. The seeds within the fruits are frequently carried great distances, and since birds usually travel from one favorable environment to another, there is a good chance the seeds will fall on fertile ground. This is an improvement on the purely random scattering by the wind.

Additionally, the digestive process facilitates germination by softening hard seed coats. The seeds of curled dock *(Rumex crispus)*, teasel *(Dipsacus sylvestris)*, and yarrow *(Achilles millefolium)* are among the seeds scattered in this way. Seed-eating and fruit-eating birds are joined in this process by squirrels, chipmunks, mice, and other small mammals, as well as larger animals such as bears, horses, moose, and deer.

Other weeds disperse their seeds by adhesion. Queen Anne's lace *(Daucus carota)*, tick-trefoil *(Desmodium* spp.), and burdock *(Arctium* spp.) are equipped with tiny hooks that snag the fur of animals as they brush against the plants. If you take your dog for a walk in a field or meadow during the autumn, you may find some of these hitchhiking seeds in its fur. You may pick up some of these seeds yourself on your jacket or pants. As you try to remove them, you will also find out how securely they attach themselves.

Winter is essential to the life cycles of many hardy plants. The seeds of these plants avoid winter cold and drought by passing through a period of dormancy. This is a precisely controlled series of events that protects against premature germination. In the dormant state, seed metabolism is reduced and growth is suspended. The length of dormancy is genetically determined; thus it persists even if environmental conditions favor germination, as they often do during the January thaw. The shift from dormancy to germination is frequently controlled by a variety of factors, including temperature, moisture, light, thickness of seed coat, enzyme activity, and growth inhibitors. Some seeds require mechanical abrasion of their seed coats as well as a period of low temperatures.

Farmers and people in the seed business know the necessary role winter plays. For certain species, they break the dormancy by putting moistened seeds under refrigeration for a few weeks. This process is called stratification. Farmers utilize natural stratification by sowing a special type of wheat in the fall. Under normal winter conditions, the seeds will germinate when the warmer weather arrives. When winters are excessively mild, however, grain yield is drastically reduced because the seeds did not experience their normal winter dormant period.

Some seeds can remain dormant for a very long time. Dock and common evening primrose (*Oenothera biennis*) were found to be dormant for one hundred years, but a Rip van Winkle in the seed world appears to be arctic lupine (*Lupinus* spp.). With the help of carbon dating, viable lupine seeds discovered in the burrows of small mammals have been estimated to be ten thousand years old. Most seeds don't sleep nearly this long, however.

Weeds and wildflowers are an essential part of the ecology in places made bare by human interference. They flourish in fallow farmlands and domestic gardens. You will find them along the margins of railroad beds and the edges of highways. These rugged wanderers also are important in the recovery of places destroyed by fires, floods, and other natural disasters, as they are able to thrive in harsh environments where other plant species cannot survive. As they grow in such places, they help to heal the wounded earth and are ultimately responsible for stabilizing plant life. The mechanisms involved in this process are not always obvious, however.

Throughout their long history, weeds have traded seed production for competitive strength and longevity. They can withstand prolonged exposure to the sun and can subsist on the offerings of nutrient-poor soil, but in the competitive arena, weeds and wildflowers generally do not fare well. After their short lives, their remains are reduced by decomposition and the nutrients locked within them are released to the surrounding soil. In normal open-field succession, shrubs such as alders and willows and tree seedlings such as gray birch eventually shade out the sun-dependent herbaceous plants—the weeds. As the shade increases and the soil improves, trees like hickories, maples, beeches, and oaks move in and acclimate themselves to the region. When this happens, as in eastern North America, a deciduous forest flourishes. In other regions of the United States, different kinds of vegetation combine to stabilize an area. In the Midwest, prairie grasses are the stabilizers of vast areas of agricultural land; in the Pacific Northwest, large conifers predominate. In the predictable succession of land plants, habitat quality inevitably changes as plants replace each other.

Through the ages, many of the plants we classify as weeds and wildflowers have been highly prized for their culinary and medicinal properties. However, their relative importance in our lives is as subject to the vagaries of the time as their seeds are to the whimsy of the wind. Today, with the emphasis on reducing the fat in our diets, there are few people who would think of cooking without flavor-enhancing herbs. Herbal medical treatments are experiencing a resurgence in popularity. Some previously despised weeds such as goldenrod and evening primrose are now highly prized plants in cultivated backyard gardens. In spite of these favorable developments, however, it seems that our love-hate relationship with weeds is destined to continue for some time.

THE WORLD OF WINTER WEEDS

What you will need	Science skills
basic kit	*observing*
collecting bag	*classifying*
trowel	*predicting*
camera	*inferring*
tangle-foot	*comparing*

OBSERVATIONS

The term *weed* is one that we have invented to describe a plant we consider useless. Most people consider weeds to be undesirable plants that are without value. They have no place beside highly prized hybrids in cultivated gardens. Some of the plants we call weeds are grown as cash crops, however. For instance, supermarket produce sections display dandelion greens along with other salad makings, but homeowners deplore the presence of the jaunty yellow flower heads of dandelions in their manicured lawns. Our ancestors ate the plant called lamb's-quarters, yet today there are few who would grow *Chenopodium album* in their gardens. Other weeds have experienced similar shifts in status over time. In this chapter, I have chosen to use the word *weeds* to apply to all of the plants that grow wild in fields and woodlands. In this sense, weeds are not our enemies.

When you go out into the fields and woods in winter, the most obvious plant life is the trees, some of them bare of leaves, others with the remains of dried leaves clinging to branches, and still others of the evergreen variety. Small plants are less obvious but usually more abundant. Since these plants lack their summer garb, identifying them presents a special challenge to the winter naturalist.

lamb's-quarters or pigweed
(Chenopodium album)

Weed Colors. Winter weeds come in a variety of subdued colors, generally some shade of brown, tan, or gray. With the help of paint chips, available wherever household paint is sold, see how many different colors and shades you can find. To add to the challenge, get a couple of friends and see who can discover the greatest variety. You will be surprised at the diversity of colors you'll find.

Botanical Terms. Knowing some botanical terms will help as you explore the world of winter weeds. Here are some of the more frequently used terms that appear in books about flowers.

Achene: A fruit containing one seed. Achenes may be equipped with silken threads that catch the wind. Distinguishing between achenes and seeds is often confusing because achenes look like seeds. Dandelions produce achenes with silken threads, but the silken threads of milkweed are attached to seeds.

Bract: A leaflike structure below the flower or inflorescence that often withers and remains throughout the winter. Frequently larger than sepals.

Calyx: A collection of sepals that are usually fused.

Capsule: A dry fruit that is generally spherical and divided into more than one section. The number of sections is frequently used to identify a winter weed.

Disk flowers: Small, tubular flowers ringed by ray flowers. Black-eyed Susan, aster, and other members of the daisy family have disk flowers.

Fruit: A seed-carrying ripened ovary, such as an apple.

Inflorescence: A shoot with clusters of flowers.

Ovary: The bottom portion of the pistil that develops into the fruit.

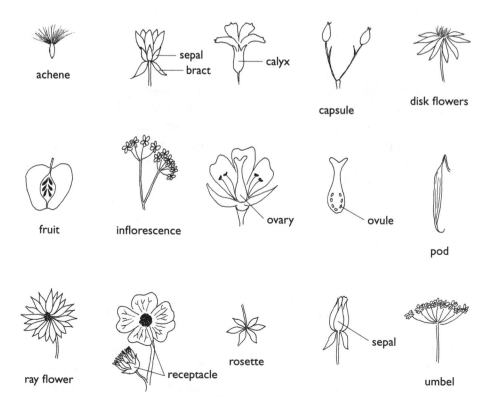

achene

sepal
bract

calyx

capsule

disk flowers

fruit

inflorescence

ovary

ovule

pod

ray flower

receptacle

rosette

sepal

umbel

Ovule: An immature, unfertilized seed.

Pistil: The female portion of the flower, which is made up of the stigma, style, and ovary. The stigma is the top part of the pistil that receives pollen. The style is the slender part of the pistil that leads to the ovary.

Pod: A woody, elongated dry fruit that opens along one or two seams.

Ray flowers: Small flowers forming a ring around the disk flowers. They are the "loves me, loves me not" flowers. Members of the daisy family have ray flowers.

Receptacle: The swollen end of a flower stalk where the flower parts such as stamens, petals, pistils, and fruits are attached. In some species, the receptacles enlarge and develop into various shapes.

Rosette: A cluster of leaves at the base of the plant, usually in a circular pattern. Mullein, tansy, and Queen Anne's lace have rosettes that persist throughout the winter.

Seeds: Formed when an ovule is fertilized by pollen. It contains the embryo (baby plant), stored food, and a protective covering.

Sepal: Usually green, these leaflike structures enclose and protect the flower buds. Many wither but remain throughout the winter at the base of the receptacle.

Umbel: A cluster of flower stalks that grows from one point at the tip of the main stem. Queen Anne's lace and other members of the parsley family such as cow parsnip, water parsnip, and sweet cicely have umbels.

Meet the Weeds. To organize the confusing world of plants, scientists have identified common properties of plants and grouped them into families according to those properties. Both common names and technical names are provided in this chapter. As you learn the meanings of the Latin names for the weeds, some of the mystery of technical nomenclature disappears. For example, the scientific name for Queen Ann's lace, *Daucus carota,* describes the carrot-parsley odor you get if you crush the leaves of the rosette. Queen Anne's lace is in the parsley family and is a wild relative of the garden carrot. The genus name for beggar-ticks, *Bidens,* refers to the two teeth on the achene, *bi* meaning "two" and *dens* meaning "tooth."

The illustrations and the text that follow will help as you begin to look for the common winter weeds in your neighborhood.

1. Aster family (Asteraceae). This family contains the largest number of flowering plants. Composites have two types of flowers: ray flowers and disk flowers. Ray flowers are flat and make up that portion of the flower head we often call the petals in asters and daisies. The ray flowers encircle the disk flowers, which are tubelike and are arranged in the center of the

flower head. The disk flowers are the black eyes of black-eyed Susans. Throughout the winter, these weeds resemble daisies without petals or with some shriveled petals remaining.

a. Goldenrod (*Solidago* spp.). Many goldenrods have plumelike flower heads that remain throughout the winter, perhaps with small, fuzzy seeds still attached. In other species the flower heads are clublike, wandlike, flat topped, or elm shaped. Look for these tall, three- to six-foot winter weeds in open fields and other sun-filled places, where they often fill large areas of open space.

b. Aster (*Aster* spp.). The delicate and wiry appearance of the winter asters helps distinguish them from their cousins, the goldenrods. Asters are not as robust looking as the goldenrods. Look for them in fields and other dry places, where their height ranges from one to seven feet.

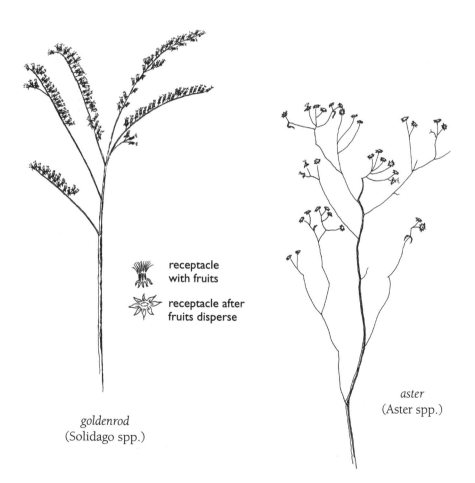

receptacle with fruits

receptacle after fruits disperse

goldenrod
(Solidago spp.)

aster
(Aster spp.)

c. Yarrow (*Achillea millefolium*). Look for the tan, flat-topped flower cluster on a smooth stem. This plant grows in fields and along roadsides and is one to three feet tall.

d. Black-eyed Susan (*Rudbeckia hirta*). Look for the black or dark brown, conelike flower heads with their black "eyes," occasionally with shriveled petals still attached. The stems, leaves, and bracts that remain are rough and hairy. You can find these plants, which grow two to three feet tall, in dry fields, open woods, and along roadways.

e. Chicory (*Cichorium intybus*). The stems of these roadside weeds have fine, vertical grooves. You may find some wedge-shaped seeds in the flower heads. The remains of the stems are about three to six feet tall.

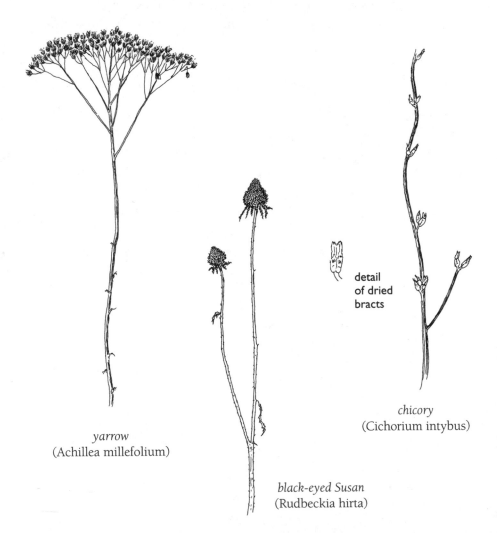

detail
of dried
bracts

yarrow
(Achillea millefolium)

black-eyed Susan
(Rudbeckia hirta)

chicory
(Cichorium intybus)

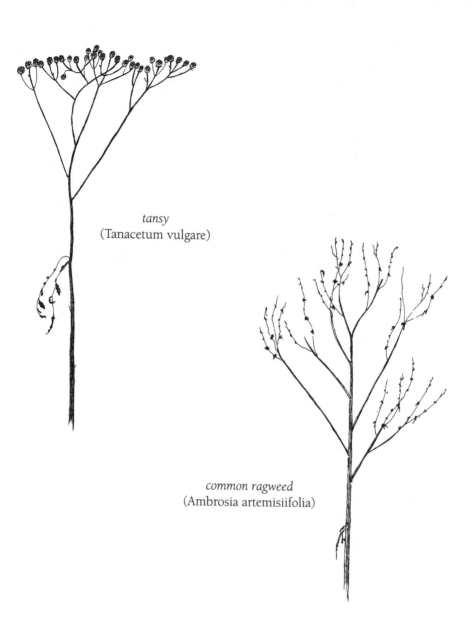

tansy
(Tanacetum vulgare)

common ragweed
(Ambrosia artemisiifolia)

f. Tansy (*Tanacetum vulgare*). Buttonlike flower heads are grouped to form a flat-topped winter weed. Crush some leaves and flower heads and you will detect a smoky smell. Look along roadsides and in fields for this one- to three-foot-tall winter weed.

g. Common ragweed (*Ambrosia artemisiifolia*). An unkempt weed with upcurving branches that you'll find in vacant lots, along roadsides, and in places recently stripped by fire or by human interference. Look for the relatively smooth three-foot stem.

joe-pye weed
(Eupatorium *spp.*)

thistle
(Cirsium spp.)

h. Thistle (*Cirsium* spp.). Even in winter you will find spines on leaves, stems, and flower heads of thistle. Some seeds with their silken threads often remain in a spiny container throughout the winter. The three- to five-foot-tall plant has a ragged appearance and is easy to find in fields and pastures and along roadways.

i. Joe-pye weed (*Eupatorium* spp.). Look for the closely grouped flower stalks, each tipped with a small white button. The weed grows about four feet tall in a variety of habitats, including wet thickets and meadows.

j. Burdock (*Arctium minus*). The flower heads are round burs covered with tiny hooked barbs. The weed grows up to five feet tall, and with its spreading branches, its width is almost equal to its height. Your dog may be the first to introduce you to this winter weed, because animals often get the burs caught in their fur.

k. Beggar-ticks (*Bidens* spp.). Each achene is a thorny, two-pronged container for a seed that can easily find its way onto your clothing or the fur of passing animals. The plants are not easy to find because they lack the showy ray flowers of other family members, but they make themselves known by hitching a ride home with you or your dog. There are several species of beggar-ticks. You will find Spanish needles (*Bidens bipinnata*), beggar-ticks or sticktights (*Bidens frondosa*), swamp beggar-ticks (*Bidens connata*), and leafy-bracted beggar-ticks (*Bidens comosa*) in roadside ditches, damp fields, and moist soil. Compare the achenes you find on your clothes with the illustrations. How many different kinds of achenes did you snare?

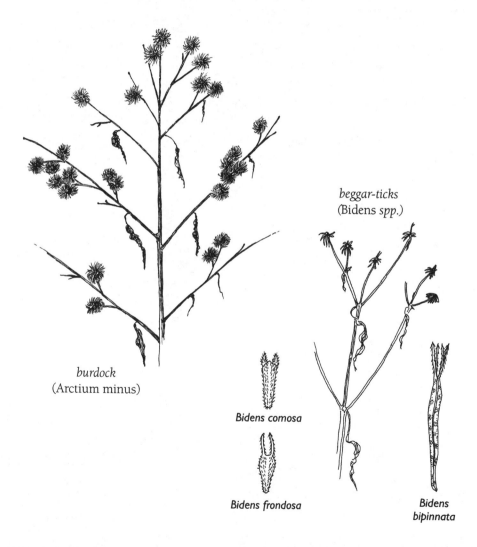

beggar-ticks
(Bidens *spp.*)

burdock
(Arctium minus)

Bidens comosa

Bidens frondosa

*Bidens
bipinnata*

2. Mustard family (Cruciferae). If the leaves remain, you will notice that the lower leaves are broad and have deep, earlike lobes. The seedpods are slender and end in a sharp "beak" that points upward. The many-seeded fruits of the various family members are shaped differently, but each fruit, regardless of its general shape, is separated by a thin membrane with seeds on each side of the membrane. When ripe, the two halves of the fruit (seedpod) split and fall off. You may find seeds still attached to the central translucent membrane that remains.

   a. Pepper grass (*Lepidium virginicum*). This winter weed can be found as a single stalk or several stalks that give it a bushy look. Look for its one- to three-foot stalks in fields and waste places. Its pods are roundish.

   b. Mustard (*Brassica* spp.). Look along roadsides and in fields for the translucent, upward-pointing membranes that divided the seedpods into two halves. The membranes are about one inch long and remain after the fruits have split and the seeds dispersed. Sometimes seeds remain attached to the membrane. Look for the black seeds of black mustard (*B. nigra*) or the white seeds of white musterd (*B. hirta*). These frequently bushy weeds grow to three feet.

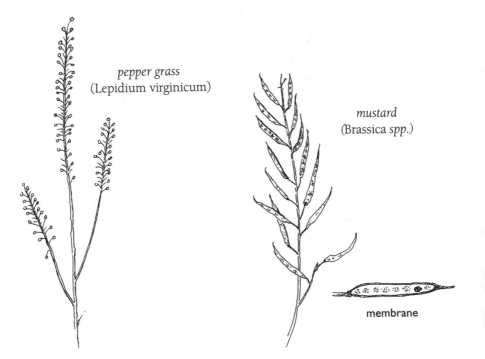

pepper grass
(Lepidium virginicum)

mustard
(Brassica *spp.*)

membrane

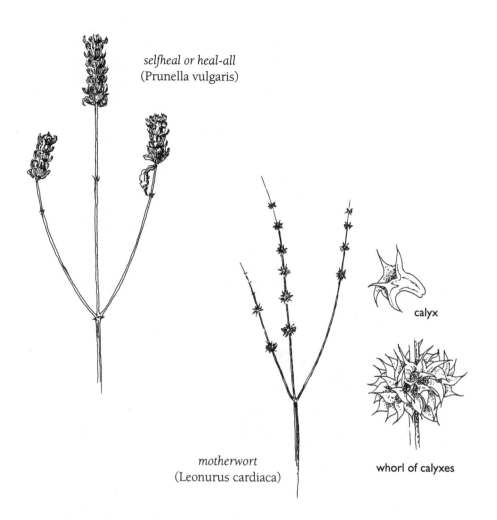

selfheal or heal-all
(Prunella vulgaris)

motherwort
(Leonurus cardiaca)

calyx

whorl of calyxes

3. Mint family (Labiatae). Most members of this family have square stems and an opposite branching pattern. Many members of this family have branches that creep along the ground and send out roots.

a. Selfheal or heal-all (*Prunella vulgaris*). The height of this winter weed varies according to its habitat. On suburban lawns, it seldom reaches more than two inches. Along roadsides and in other waste places, however, it can reach a height of three feet.

b. Motherwort (*Leonurus cardiaca*). During the growing season, you can see the whorled arrangement of the leaves and flowers. In the winter, however, you will see only the dried calyxes (fused sepals), which circle the stem at intervals along its length. Look for motherwort in waste places, where it grows to four feet.

4. Saint-John's-wort family (Guttiferae). Members of this family have opposite branches that curve upward. Their fruits are three-parted capsules.
   a. Saint-John's-wort *(Hypericum perforatum)*. Look for the upcurved,
      opposite branches. You can find this one- to three-foot plant in fields
      and meadows and along roadsides.
5. Loosestrife family (Lythraceae). The fruit capsules of family members are
   loosely whorled around the stem.
   a. Purple loosestrife *(Lythrum salicaria)*. Easily recognizable by its open,
      airy shape and opposite branching pattern. If the fruits remain on the
      branches, they will be in a whorled pattern. Purple loosestrife is not a
      native plant. It is an aggressive nuisance species with few antagonists.
      It grows in wet, marshy places and has spread across the land with
      unbridled energy, pushing out native species. It grows from four to six
      feet tall and is distinguished by bright purple-red flowers throughout
      the summer.

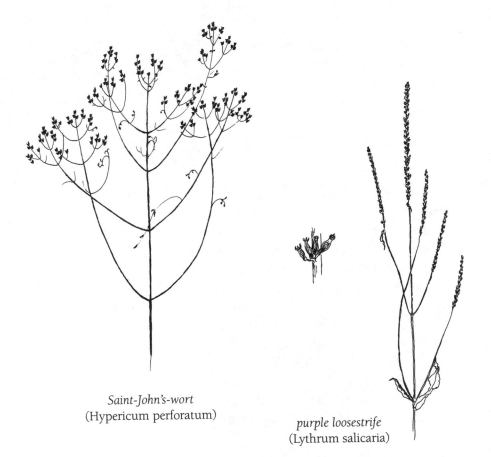

Saint-John's-wort
(Hypericum perforatum)

purple loosestrife
(Lythrum salicaria)

common milkweed
(Asclepias syriaca)

tick-trefoil
(Desmodium *spp.*)

6. Milkweed family (Asclepiadacea). The fruits of family members are woody pods, and the seeds within the pods are equipped with fine, silk-like hairs.

   a. Milkweed (*Asclepias* spp.). The bumpy, woody pods of this plant are swollen at the base and taper to a point at the top. The pods slit open down the middle to expose the flat, brown seeds, each with silken hollow filaments attached. The plant grows three to five feet tall.

7. Pea family (Leguminosae). Seedpods of family members are bilaterally symmetrical and open along one or two seams like a peapod. The seeds hang from the pod like peas.

   a. Tick-trefoil (*Desmodium* spp.). Tiny pods covered with fine, hairy hooks are seen more frequently on your clothes or pets than on the plants. The multisectioned pods often form chains while they are on the plant. Open a pod to find the lima-bean-shaped seed inside. A hand lens will help you see the detail on the pods. The weed grows to six feet in meadows, thickets, and, most frequently, wooded areas.

8. Teasel family (Dipsacaceae). Small flowers in cramped, prickly heads characterize members of this family. In winter only the bristly heads remain.

    a. Teasel (*Dipsacus sylvestris*). Spiny, egg-shaped seed containers and spiny bracts that curve up alongside the "eggs" are characteristic of this plant. Its stem also is prickly. The first-year rosette, which persists through the winter, is easy to identify. Look for bristly hairs on green leaves that resemble seersucker. Seeds mature in the head of the teasel; try to shake some out.

9. Dogbane family (Apocynaceae). Members of this family have woody pods that reveal close ties to the milkweed family and five-lobed, bell-shaped flowers. During the growing season, the plant stems exude a milky liquid if broken.

    a. Spreading dogbane (*Apocynum androsaemifolium*). Slender, woody pods ranging in length from three to eight inches dangle in pairs from the plant. Silky threads attached to small, brown seeds within the pods are another trait dogbane shares with milkweeds. Dogbane grows from one to four feet. Look for it in thickets and along roadways.

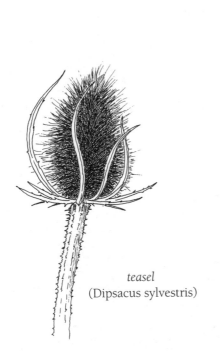

teasel
(Dipsacus sylvestris)

dogbane
(Apocynum androsaemifolium)

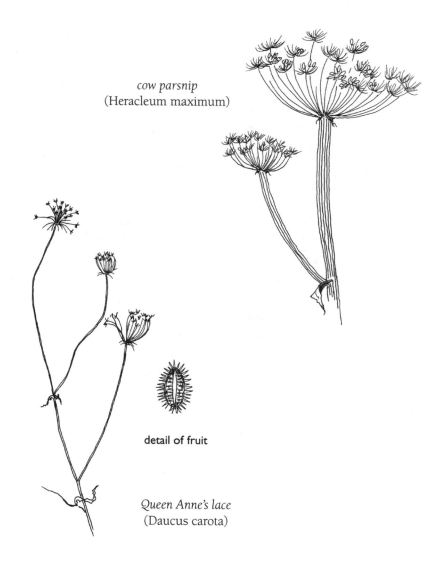

cow parsnip
(Heracleum maximum)

detail of fruit

Queen Anne's lace
(Daucus carota)

10. Parsley family (Umbelliferae). Characteristic of this family is the umbel, in which all flower stalks emanate from a single point on the stem. The fruits mature in umbels that frequently resemble inside-out umbrellas.

   a. Queen Anne's lace *(Daucus carota)*. Look for winter rosettes of lacy fuzzy leaves and for the grooved flower stalks and seeds that are characteristic of this family.

   b. Cow parsnip *(Heracleum maximum)*. This gigantic version of Queen Anne's lace is difficult to miss. It grows to about nine feet tall on a hollow, deeply grooved stem. Look for it where the soil is damp during the growing season.

11. Buckwheat family (Polygonaceae). Wraparound leaf scars are typical of this family. They remain on the stem after the leaf falls off, sometimes leaving a swelling on the stem. Three-winged fruits are characteristic.
    a. Curled dock (*Rumex crispus*). Grows in fields and meadows and along the side of the road. You may find it as tall as three feet. Look for its deep, rich copper color and characteristic shape that make dock easy to spot in the winter landscape.
12. Snapdragon family (Scrophulariaceae). The two-parted capsule that looks like a turtle's head is a common characteristic of the snapdragon family.
    a. Mullein (*Verbascum thapsus*). Mullein is common and grows in dry, rocky, and open areas such as gravelly roadsides, abandoned construction sites, and the edges of fields. Its characteristic single, fuzzy stalk can grow to six feet. Look for the pale green, thick, hairy rosettes that are easy to find in the winter where snow does not cover them. The stalk may be the only sign of mullein if snow covers the ground, and you may have to push aside the snow to find the telltale rosette.
13. Mallow family (Malvaceae). The fruits of this family are frequently five-parted capsules or may be circular pods with many sections. Soft, fuzzy stems are characteristic of some family members.

fruit

dock
(Rumex crispus)

common mullein
(Verbascum thapsus)

velvet-leaf
(Abutilon theophrasti)

a. Velvet-leaf (*Abutilon theophrasti*). Stem and sepals are velvety. Look for the spool-like capsule. Thin membranes divide the capsule into pie-shaped wedges. The edges of the capsule are beaklike and the bottom is hairy.

Clues to Winter Identification. When left with only empty seed containers and gray-brown stalks, many people wait until the next growing season to find out the identity of the winter weeds in their neighborhood. But there is no need to put off learning about the diversity that exists in the world of winter weeds. This activity will help you focus on some features of common weeds that are readily observable. *Weeds in Winter,* by Lauren Brown (see the Bibliography), will guide you further.

From October to April, the dried flower stalks, withered leaves, and seedpods give some clues as to the plants' identity. First examine the stem. Is it smooth and velvety like velvet-leaf, is it rough and fuzzy like mullein, or does it have prickers like teasel? Cut across the stem with a knife. If it is square, the weed may be a member of the mint family. A three-sided stem on a grass plant tells you it is a sedge.

Also note whether the branches are opposite each other on the stem, as in the mint and Saint-John's-wort families.

Next, look for seedpods and study them. Are they barbed as in burdock or winged as in dock? Shake a stem of mullein over some snow or other uncluttered surface, and you may create a shower of seeds.

Do leaves remain on the weed? Depending on their condition, you may be able to see fine or stiff hairs on them.

Crush various parts of the weed. If there is an odor of parsley or carrot, the plant may be Queen Anne's lace. A smoky odor may indicate that it is a member of the daisy family.

What kind of root system does it have? You'll find a yellowish white carrotlike root if you dig up a Queen Anne's lace rosette. Mullein and burdock also have taproots. Thistle sends out creeping roots with underground buds. Can you figure out the advantages of these different root systems? What do the different root systems tell you about the plants' habitats? (See Chapter Note 1.)

When you find a few weeds that interest you, write descriptions of them in your field notebook. Make a sketch or take a photograph of each weed. Indicate where you found them, the date, and the weather conditions. You can return to this place during the growing season and find out about the soil conditions and what other plants are growing in the area. You can make a fine science project based on winter weeds and their niches.

What Do Weeds Tell about the Habitat? The presence of specific winter weeds tells you something about the place where they grow. For example, mullein indicates that the habitat is generally hot and dry during the summer. The presence of burdock tells you the field has been abandoned for several years. Cattails (*Typha* spp.) indicate a wet habitat, and common evening primrose a dry one. Tall wormwood (*Artemisia campestris*) grows on beaches and dunes.

Life Histories. Winter weeds are herbaceous plants. Unlike the woody stems and trunks of shrubs and trees that persist throughout the winter, herbaceous plants are characterized by nonwoody stems. At the end of each growing season, the stems and other plant parts that live above the ground die. Plant materials that decorate the winter landscape are the remnants of herbaceous plants.

One of three different life cycles is illustrated by each winter weed species. Some herbaceous plants that make up populations of our winter weeds are classified as annuals. These plants complete their life cycle in a single growing season; their leaves, stems, flower parts, and root systems die at the end of each growing season. The next generation survives the winter as dormant seeds. Beggar-ticks and pepper grass are annuals that adorn the winter landscape.

Biennials have a two-year cycle from seed to death. During their first year, biennials produce roots, stems, and leaves (vegetative growth), usually a characteristic rosette of leaves lying close to the ground that persists over the winter. Food manufactured during the spring and summer is stored in the root

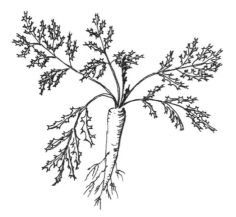

Queen Anne's lace root and winter rosette
(Daucus carota)

A winter rosette of teasel
(Dipsacus *spp.*)

systems during the cold season. The second year, energy is put into the growth of reproductive structures—the flowers, fruits, and seeds. Once these plants have reproduced, their life ends. Queen Anne's lace and teasel are examples of biennials.

Perennials live for an indefinite period of time. They can live from a few years to a few hundred years. Once they have reached maturity, they produce seeds regularly or even intermittently until they die. New growth dies back at the end of each season but the roots continue to live. Perennials that persist as winter weeds include tansy, joe-pye weed, and heal-all.

Below is a list of weeds that illustrate each life cycle. Look for them the next time you are outdoors on a winter day.

Annuals	Biennials	Perennials
beggar-ticks	black-eyed Susan	curled dock
cocklebur	burdock	goldenrod
pepper grass	common evening primrose	tansy
ragweed	common mullein (has a rosette)	hemp dogbane
	teasel (has a rosette)	yarrow
	Queen Anne's lace (has a rosette)	chicory
		heal-all
		joe-pye weed
		common milkweed
		tick-trefoil
		purple loosestrife

EXPLORATIONS

Seeds and Fruits. A seed is produced when pollen and egg unite in the process of fertilization. Each seed contains an embryo (baby plant) and its food supply, which are surrounded by a protective covering, or coat. A fruit is a mature ovary that contains seeds. Melons are fruits because they are ripened ovaries that contain seeds. Although we generally refer to tomatoes as vegetables, they are fruits because they are also ripened ovaries that contain seeds.

As you explore the world of winter weeds, you will find plants bearing pods. Pods are specialized seed-bearing fruits. Some of the pods will be in reasonably good condition, but others will be torn and ragged from beatings by wind and weather.

When mature, some fruits break open and release their seeds. Other plants shed their fruits while the seeds are still in them. Achenes, one-seeded fruits, are often difficult for the beginner to distinguish from seeds because they frequently resemble seeds.

If you find a thistle flower head, remove several achenes with fuzz tightly gathered. Put the achenes in a warm, dry place free from even the slightest breeze. How long does it take for the fuzz to open?

With the help of a hand lens, look closely at the silk threads of milkweed and thistle. How are the threads different? Are they separate? Branched? Do you think the difference will affect resistance to wind? You can check your prediction through a simple investigation. Get some milkweed seeds and thistle achenes. With the help of a friend, drop one of each from a height of six feet. How long does it take for each to reach the ground? Repeat this several times and record the data on a chart similar to the one that follows.

Hint: Be sure to conduct this experiment in a place free of the slightest breeze.

FLUFF DESIGN AND SPEED OF FALL

Weed	Drop Height	Trial No.	Time in Seconds
Milkweed	6 feet	1.	
		2.	
		3.	
Thistle	6 feet	1.	
		2.	
		3.	

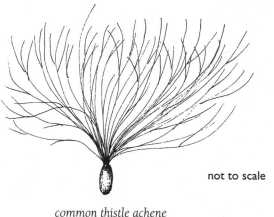

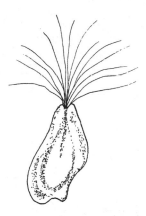

not to scale

common thistle achene
(Cirsium vulgare)

swamp-milkweed seed
(Asclepias incarnata)

Open the dry flower head of burdock. Are the seeds dispersed by animals or wind? How many achenes (seeds) are there within the bur (fruit)? How do they get out?

How Many Seeds? Based on the huge number of seeds produced by weeds, it is obvious that these rugged plants put a great deal of energy into reproduction. You can find out approximately how many seeds a winter weed produces by counting them. A milkweed pod would be a good place to begin. Open the pod along the seam, and you will find the seeds arranged like shingles on a roof. Count them. Count the seeds in a few other pods from different milkweed plants, if you can find them. What is the average number of seeds produced by your sample of pods? How many milkweed plants are there in the area? How many milkweed seeds are produced in that place? Try this simple method for some other weed species. Are you convinced that weeds have the potential for producing prolific numbers of offspring?

Find a Queen Anne's lace flower head. The fruits of this common winter weed are found in every tiny umbel that makes up the large umbel blossom, which most people identify as the flower. One person tallied 34 umbels, which contained a total of 782 spiny fruits. How many tiny umbels and fruits do you count?

A Seed and Fruit Collection. Collect seeds and fruits from many different winter weeds and make a display of them. Record the location of the weeds that produced the seeds and fruits. This is especially helpful if you want to return to find out the identity of the weed. Describe each seed or fruit. A hand lens will help you see detail. Your display will illustrate the range of variation in seed size, design, and adaptation for dispersal.

There is a direct relationship between the size of a seed and the amount of food stored in it. Species with large seeds generally produce relatively fewer seeds than those that produce small seeds. What plant produced the smallest seed? The largest seed? Was one shape more common than others?

Put the seeds from each different weed in a separate plastic sandwich bag. Label the bags so that you will know which weeds the seeds are from. Later you can attach the seeds to the appropriate place on your display. Draw or photograph each weed to show the unique characteristics of each seed and fruit in your collection. As you examine the seed, you will become aware of the technique each one has for its dispersal. Do they have hooks that will catch on animal fur, tufts of threads, or paper-thin winged membranes that will catch the wind? The chart below will help organize your collection of seeds and fruits.

SEED COLLECTION

Weed	Type of Fruit or Seed	Description	Agent of Dispersal
Queen Anne's lace			
Milkweed	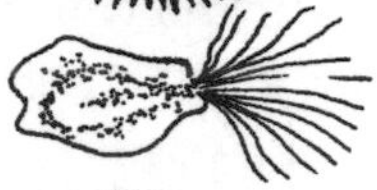		
Dock			
Burdock			
Beggar-ticks			
Joe-pye weed	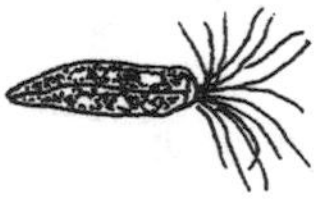		
Mullein			
Pepper grass	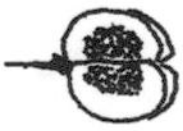		
Tansy			

Add to the list any other winter weeds you find as you explore the world of seeds and fruits. It is said that weeds that produce the most seeds also produce the smallest ones. What do you think?

A Weed Collection. Winter weeds can make lovely displays. Collect some weeds that you find especially beautiful and exhibit them for your friends and family. Some interesting ones are velvet-leaf, daisy fleabane, heal-all, and pepper grass. Your collection could feature specific plant families, such as the Buckwheat family or composite (daisy) family, or it could show a mix of families. This is an excellent opportunity to discover additional winter weeds.

Build a Seed Collector. Build a seed collector similar to the one in the diagram. Smear nondrying, sticky Tanglefoot on the plastic covering on the seed collector. Tanglefoot can be found at hardware, garden-supply, or farm

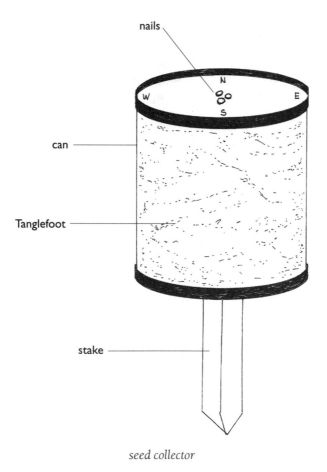

seed collector

feed stores. *Caution:* Tanglefoot is very difficult to remove from skin and clothing. Silicone grease on glass plates will trap airborne pollen and also should work for most herbaceous seeds. This arrangement may be easier to use than Tanglefoot. Set the pole of your seed collector in the snow or soil so that the collecting surface is about a foot above the surface of the ground. Orient the direction markers on the collector with the earth's magnetic field. You may need to use a compass.

After several days, retrieve your collector. Before you do so, predict which seeds you are most likely to find on its surface. How do your predictions line up with what you collected? From what compass direction did the most seeds arrive?

With the help of your field notes, count and record the number of seeds from each type of weed. You may want to use a hand lens to get a good view of your seeds and to omit any debris such as leaf litter that might have been transported by the wind to your collector.

Which were the most common and the least common weed seeds? Which weed species is the most likely to provide food for the birds? Small mammals? You can get a general idea based on the size of the seeds and the quantity of those seeds on your collector. Are there weeds, such as thistle, that supply downy nesting material? What was the direction of the prevailing wind during the time of your collection? Make a tally sheet similar to the one below.

A TALLY OF WIND DISPERSED SEEDS

Method	Number
Wings	
Silk threads	
Other (describe)	

Have a friend erect a seed collector a few miles away from yours. Compare your findings. What similarities and differences did you find? What might account for the differences in your findings?

CHAPTER NOTE

1. Plants have either fibrous roots or taproots. Fibrous root systems are made up of many branches of fibrous tissue that intertwine among the soil particles. They grow relatively close to the surface, where they absorb miner-

als and water as it begins to percolate into the soil. Grasses are plants with this kind of root system.

Taproot systems contain only one large, rapidly growing root that penetrates deep into the soil. They are good anchors for plants growing in loose soil or in windy places. Taproots draw minerals and water from sources deep beneath the soil.

CHAPTER 7

Insects

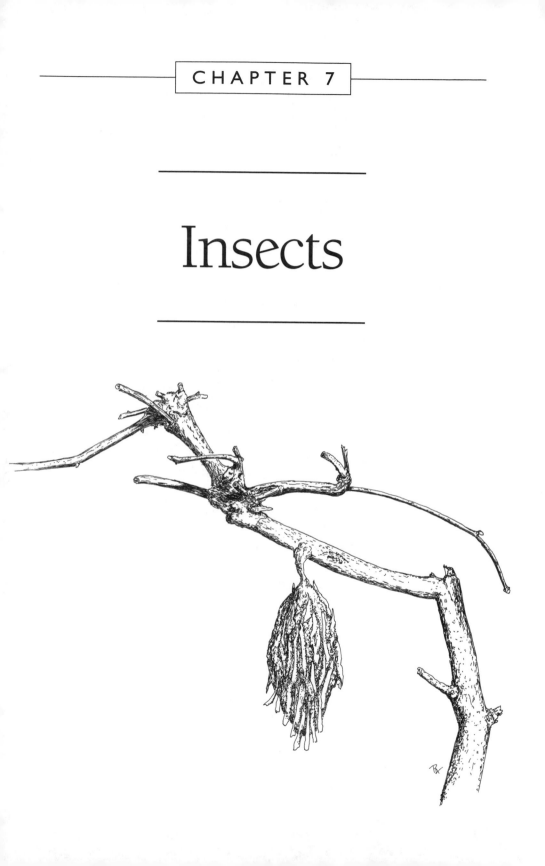

THE DANCE OF THE SNOW BUGS

The calendar tells us February is the last full month of winter. Although snow may still cover the ground, a subtle sense of spring is in the air. The days are noticeably longer, attic wasps make their appearance in our homes, and seed catalogs arrive in our mailboxes. During these warming days, the snow around tree trunks seems to come alive. If you use skis or snowshoes to make your way through the snow-covered landscape, you may have witnessed the dance of the snow bugs. Pepperlike specks on the snow appear and then disappear. The movement occurs so swiftly that it makes the surface of the snow seem fluid. If you put your hand into this "living snow," the tiny "pepper grains" will leap on and off without leaving a clue as to where they went.

You have witnessed the surface activity of insects called springtails. They are nicknamed snowfleas. Signaled by the right combination of temperature and humidity, these minute insects move up from the soil in huge numbers to the snow's surface around tree trunks and rocks where the snow is partially melted away. They have spent the coldest days of winter beneath the soil litter, feeding on decaying plant material, bits of fungi, and bacteria.

Catching a springtail takes very little skill but a great deal of determination and patience. One way to trap some of these tiny insects is to roll them into a snowball and put it into a sandwich bag. When it is convenient, put some of the bug-packed snow into a bug box (a plastic container with a magnifier in the lid) and examine it carefully. You may be able to see the usual insect traits—one pair of feelers, three pairs of legs attached to the chest or thorax, and three body divisions: head, thorax, and abdomen. You will notice, however, that springtails lack wings. You may also discover that some are hairy but others are covered with scales. The presence of only four to six abdominal segments has caused some discussion among scientists as to whether springtails are true insects or should be placed in another group of living things; perhaps a group of their own.

Wingless springtails (*Achorutes nivicola*) belong to a very old and established line of insects called Collembola, which originated before wings had evolved. From an evolutionary point of view, Collembola have been highly successful. The measure of success for any living species is simple: Each generation needs to survive long enough to reproduce. If this short-term success is maintained for, say, 100 million years, we can say that the species is highly successful.

The name Collembola comes from Greek words meaning "glue peg" and refers to a tube that grows on the underside of the springtail's abdomen. Under laboratory conditions, scientists have observed springtails inserting the glue

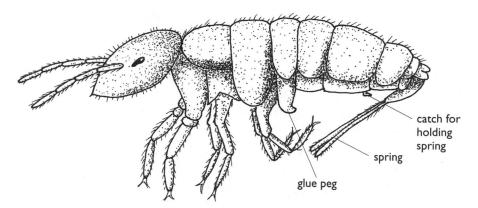

catch for
holding
spring

spring

glue peg

Springtails (Collembola) live in the surface layer of soil and leaf litter.

pegs into drops of moisture when the air around them is dry. The drier the air, the more frequently the springtails dip their glue pegs into the moisture droplets. This method of obtaining emergency drinking water is an important survival strategy.

Moving from place to place and escaping predators are problems that face all insects. Springtails have their own solution to these problems. With the help of a mechanism responsible for their common name, they leap. The tiny insects accomplish this by folding a pair of modified legs under their abdomen. The legs are held in place by hooklike structures. When the hooks relax, the legs spring against anything solid (even a snow crystal), catapulting the creature into the air for a distance of about eight inches. This is a remarkable feat, since the insect is only about one-sixteenth inch long.

Not all springtails are equipped with this launching device. It is found on those that live in the soil surface in the leaf litter. Close relatives that live within deeper layers of soil do not have this elegant structure, but you are not likely to find these blind white or gray creatures, since they are very small and inconspicuous.

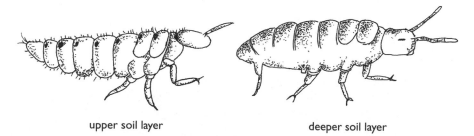

upper soil layer

deeper soil layer

Different types of springtails are found below the surface of the soil.

Most of the bugs that are the stars of the snow dance are brown or gray, but many are yellow, red, orange, or purple. The bright colors warn predators such as ants, their primary enemies, that springtails are foul tasting. One encounter with these colorful insects is enough to keep experienced predators from dining on springtails.

Springtails reach the peak of their activity toward the end of winter. They mate in early spring, and by summer, eggs that were laid beneath the soil hatch. The emerging springtail nymphs look like adults, only smaller. They develop through a series of molts, or shedding of outer skin, until they reach adult size. At this point, there are no further molts and the springtails are capable of reproduction. This kind of development is called a series-of-molts life cycle.

In contrast, butterflies and moths develop through a four-stage life cycle, or complete metamorphosis. They begin life in eggs that have been deposited by an adult female. Caterpillars, or larvae, hatch from the eggs. The larvae are more like worms, not at all like the adults. After an eating frenzy, the larva spins a cocoon around itself where it continues its development toward adulthood. At this stage it is called a pupa. Eventually the butterfly or moth emerges.

Dragonflies and stoneflies have a three-stage life cycle, or incomplete metamorphosis. The young that hatch from the eggs look like small copies of the adults, except that their heads are large and they are wingless. Through a series of molts, the nymphs eventually become full-sized adults with wings.

The most astonishing fact about springtails is that they are the most abundant of all land insects, numbering hundreds of thousands per acre. Scientists have discovered about two thousand species. You can find them in almost any moist soil, under stones, beneath fallen timbers, and in the crevices of loose tree bark. As long as moisture and food requirements are met, springtails will inhabit every conceivable location, from sea level to mountaintop, from the tropics to Antarctica.

Their obscurity probably lies in the fact that they don't bother us. They don't bite us or our pets. They don't eat the wood supports of our homes or our prized woolens. They don't invade our kitchens. They don't buzz, squeak, or whistle.

Although some springtails are cannibalistic, most of them feed on dead leaf material that has been softened by molds and decay bacteria found in the soil. The moist areas around tree trunks and the stems of woody plants are rich feeding grounds for them. Dead leaves and grasses contain minerals and organic matter such as sugars and starches. Springtails eat these materials and convert them into the proteins of their own bodies. What is not used is excreted in a modified form that can be used as fertilizer by trees and other plants. Because the protein of the springtails is a rich food for other insects and small animals, they are a very important link in the food chain. The dance of the snow bugs represents a celebration of that great web of life that will soon once again fill our woods with sound and motion.

THE WORLD OF WINTER INSECTS

What you will need

basic kit

thermometer

wide-mouth jar

Burlese funnel (see text)

screening

trowel

bucket

Science skills

observing

recording

comparing

experimenting

OBSERVATIONS

Most of us give very little thought to insects in the winter. Where they go and how they survive the cold weather is not always clear, yet we do know that insect species endure winter in one or another stage of their life cycle.

Some of those insects that undergo complete metamorphosis spend the winter as undeveloped eggs, others as larvae or as pupae. Some even overwinter in the adult stage. Those that undergo incomplete metamorphosis have a smaller range of winter strategies.

In the activities that follow, you will have an opportunity to explore your neighborhood for overwintering insects and learn about the various strategies that insects have developed to survive the cold.

Overwintering Insects. Many insects spend the winter as fertilized eggs, and others as larvae. Fewer insect species pass the winter as pupae, and an even smaller number hibernate as adults. In this activity, you will become aware of the many places where insects at various stages in their life cycles spend the winter. Beginning naturalists often like to know the name of the larva that made the cocoon, the species that laid the eggs on the cherry tree, or the moth or butterfly that a caterpillar will become. This is not a require-

Complete metamorphosis

eastern tent caterpillar moth
(Malacosoma americanum)

5. The adult moth emerges.

1. The female lays a band of eggs around a small twig and covers them with a foamy brown substance that hardens and protects the eggs over the winter.

4. The pupating caterpillar leaves the tent and makes a thin, creamy to pale yellow cocoon on or near the host plant. The pupa is often visible inside.

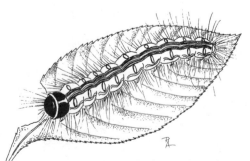

2. The larvae hatch in the spring and form silky tents in the crotches of tree limbs.

3. They feed outside their tents, using them only for resting. They grow by molting.

Incomplete metamorphosis

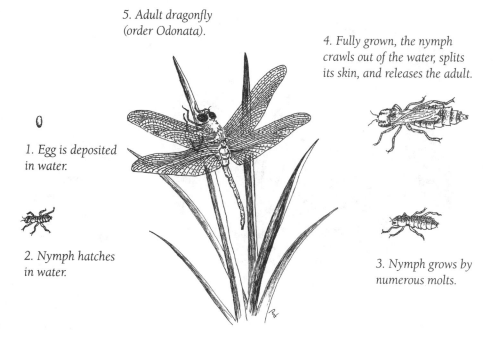

5. Adult dragonfly
(order Odonata).

4. Fully grown, the nymph
crawls out of the water, splits
its skin, and releases the adult.

1. Egg is deposited
in water.

2. Nymph hatches
in water.

3. Nymph grows by
numerous molts.

ment for learning some fascinating things about insects and the winter, however. The following are the overwintering stages of some insects.

Eggs. Many insects overwinter as fertilized eggs in which development has been suspended until conditions favor growth. You can begin your search for eggs after the leaves fall and continue it through the winter.

1. During the spring, tent caterpillars (Lasiocampid family of moths) live in cottony masses in the crotches of tree branches, especially on apple and cherry trees. These "tents" are home to hundreds of larvae, or caterpillars, which feed on the tender young leaves of the tree. Keep track of the trees that host these tents. In the winter, you will find hard, shiny, capsule-shaped egg masses bundled around twigs of apple, wild cherry, and related trees. The egg masses often resemble globs of varnish.

2. Needles of white pine (*Pinus strobus*) are host to thousands of minute eggs covered by white scales, which make the needles look as though they have a dusting of snow.

3. Bagworm moths spend the winter as eggs in cocoonlike sacks that dangle from evergreen shrubs and trees by silken threads. Collect a few bags and open them. The cocoon of a female bagworm will hold hundreds of yel-

A. Eggs of the tent caterpillar moth form a shiny mass around twigs of fruit trees.

C. Eggs of the bagworm moth overwinter in the parents' bags.

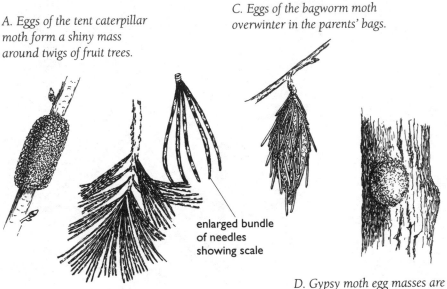

enlarged bundle
of needles
showing scale

B. White scales protect the eggs of the pine-needle coccid.

D. Gypsy moth egg masses are straw colored and covered with scales from the moth's body.

low eggs. The larvae that make the bags are not easily seen; they live in the ground, where they thrive on grass or roots.

4. Gypsy moths (*Lymantria dispar*) spend the winter as eggs. Look for their straw-colored masses on tree trunks, especially the trunks of oaks.

Larvae.

1. The larva of the cat-tail moth (*Arzama obliqua*) spends the winter in stalks of cattails.

2. Look for the banded woolly bear caterpillar sheltered under leaves and grasses. In spring, it forms a cocoon and emerges as the Isabella moth (*Isia isabella*).

3. The maple-leaf cutter larva lives in fallen maple leaves. Look for the small white patch on a maple leaf. Hold the leaf to the light, and you may see the larva moving inside. The black specks are wastes from the larva.

Pupae. Each species designs a cocoon that is unique to it. Experienced naturalists can identify the insect by examining the cocoon.

1. The papery, silky, pod-shaped cocoon of the cecropia moth, one of the giant silkworm moths (family Saturniidae), contains the pupal stage of this

insect. The cocoons are attached lengthwise to the undersides of twigs of the trees on which the caterpillars have fed.

2. The common cabbage butterflies in the Pieridae family spend the winter in cocoons, which you will find on objects near their summer food. Larvae in this family feed on cabbage, clover, shepherd's purse, and related plants.

Some insects overwinter as larvae.

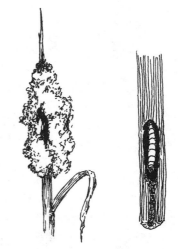

Woolly bear hibernating under leaf litter.

The larvae of the cat-tail moth overwinter in seedheads and stalks.

Winterproof pupa

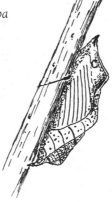

The pod-shaped papery cocoon of the cecropia moth is hard to see because it blends in with the branches.

The cabbage butterfly pupae store glycerol in their body fluids and have been known to survive to -22°F.

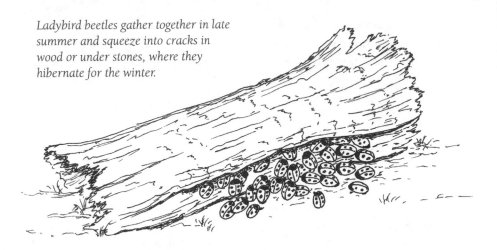

Ladybird beetles gather together in late summer and squeeze into cracks in wood or under stones, where they hibernate for the winter.

Adult. There are not many insect species that spend the winter months as adults.

1. Adult mourning cloak butterflies (*Nymphalis antiopa*) spend the cold weather under loose tree bark or beneath roof shingles. In these places, only the brown scales on their wings can be seen, so they are difficult to find. Their blackish wings with yellow borders are not visible when the butterfly is snug in its winter home. Look for them where willows or elms grow, or around apple orchards where dried fruit remains on the trees. They can also be found around cider mills.

2. Ladybird beetles, or ladybugs (family Coccinellidae), pass the cold months huddled in large masses under fallen logs, felled branches, piles of leaves, and rocks, where they feed on plant material.

3. Pill bugs, or sow bugs, are actually crustaceans and not insects. These gray creatures roll into tight, round balls when disturbed. Look for them beneath stones and decaying leaf litter. You will notice they have seven pairs of leglike appendages rather than the six pairs of legs that characterize insects.

Finding Overwintering Insects. It takes careful observation to find over-wintering insects. Look for egg cases on bare branches of trees and shrubs. Pupae dangle from the bare branches of deciduous trees and shrubs and from twigs of evergreens. Check beneath the thin surface layer of soil, under decaying leaves, in log piles, and between chunks of loose tree bark. Don't forget the woodpile. This is a favorite of termites, wood-boring beetles, and crickets.

Make a chart that shows where you found each insect and whether it was an egg, larva, pupa, or adult. Write descriptions of your finds. Remember, the names of the insects are not important.

OVERWINTERING INSECTS

Location	Insect Stage				Comments
	Egg	Larva	Pupa	Adult	
Bare branches					
Under stones					
Under leaves					
Under logs					
Under tree bark					
Woodpile					
Soil					

Other Signs of Insects. A variety of bark beetles etch evidence of their presence on the surface of dead trees and fallen logs. Females carve the tunnels and lay eggs in them. The emerging larvae eat their way through the bark and contribute to the network of tunnels.

Winter Shelter. Many insects spend the winter in rotting logs and old tree stumps. Find out how warm it is in these places by putting a thermometer into a rotting log or stump on a cold day and leaving it there for a few minutes. How does the temperature in this "winter home" compare with the temperature outside? Check the temperature inside a pile of rotting leaves. How does it compare with the temperature of the air and the log or stump? Look for a hole in a tree and repeat your investigation. If you were a bug, which place would you spend the cold months?

Many types of bark beetle (Scolytidae) tunnels may be found by peeling away the bark of dead trees or fallen logs.

EXPLORATIONS

Insects are cold-blooded. This means that their internal temperature is regulated by the temperature of their external environment. Insects' metabolic rates respond to the cold by slowing down. This causes the insect, at any stage in its development, to become dormant.

There are two forms of dormancy: quiescence and diapause. Quiescence is a short-term event in which the insect responds to temporary changes in weather conditions. Diapause is a long-term dormancy. It is an overwintering strategy controlled by both daylight and temperature, though light seems to be the critical variable. During diapause, the insect remains in a state of lowered metabolic activity, until days lengthen and there is enough light to trigger hormonal activity, causing the insect to awaken. Different species of insects enter diapause as eggs, larvae, pupae, or adults.

Air Temperature and Insect Activity. You can find out how quiescence works with some help from an ant, a bug box or other container, and a refrigerator. This experiment must be done when ants are still active.

Capture an ant in the container. Determine the temperature inside the refrigerator and record it in your field notebook. Put the container with the ant into the refrigerator. How long does it take for the ant to cease movement and become quiescent? After you take the container out of the refrigerator, how long does it take the ant to resume its normal activity? Would a change in the cooling temperature (in the freezer, or longer in the refrigerator) affect the behavior of the ant? Try it.

Compare the amount of time one insect requires to recover from various temperature intervals with that of others of the same species.

You can try this investigation with other insects that use quiescent strategies, such as crickets, roaches, or termites. Compare your results for different species.

Galls. Galls are benign growths on plant tissue that may result when an adult female insect lays its eggs on a plant. Some insects lay their eggs on the surface of a plant part; others make a hole in a plant part and lay their eggs inside. The exact nature of gall formation is not yet known. It is known that insects secrete growth-regulating chemicals called auxins. In response to the auxins secreted by an egg-laying female or by the larva that develops from the egg, the plant either produces new cells or enlarges some of the existing cells. The result is a gall unique to the insect that caused it.

The inner walls of the gall are rich in proteins supplied by the plant. The developing larva can also secrete an enzyme that converts plant starch into energy-rich sugar. Species whose larval form has a jaw mechanism for chewing

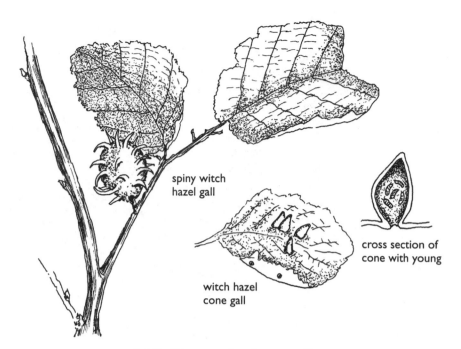

spiny witch
hazel gall

witch hazel
cone gall

cross section of
cone with young

Aphids (Homoptera) make open galls.

can tear and munch tender plant cells. Larval species equipped with piercing or sucking mouthparts can drink their nourishment.

The newly developed gall protects the larva from sun, wind, rain, and predators, but it doesn't necessarily provide security. Scores of small, hungry insect and mite predators hunt for occupied galls. Some don't attack the larvae but compete for the food inside the galls, which can cause the larvae to starve. Other interlopers don't kill the larvae but parasitize them. Sometimes even parasites of the parasites find their way into the gall. Some creatures will make a gall their home after they have eaten all the inhabitants. If the gall is big enough—and some grow as large as baseballs—even small birds will move in after the mayhem has ceased.

Winter is an ideal time to look for galls. Trees, shrubs, and weed stalks bare of leaves make gall hunts rewarding. More than 90 percent of all galls form on plant leaves, but they also may form on branches, twigs, buds, flowers, fruits, and even roots. They exist in a variety of sizes, shapes, and colors. Examine the galls you find. How big are they? Are all the galls of the same type also the same size? What shape are they—round, oval, egg or football shaped? Some galls have very odd shapes. They may look like tubes or buttons. Many are simply globs of woody material. What color are they? Are they

Pine cone willow galls are the home of a single orange fly maggot but may house a great variety of long- and short-term "boarders."

Blackberry knot gall—a multiple structure made by the cynipid wasp larvae.

Mossy rose galls are multicellular galls made by cynipids.

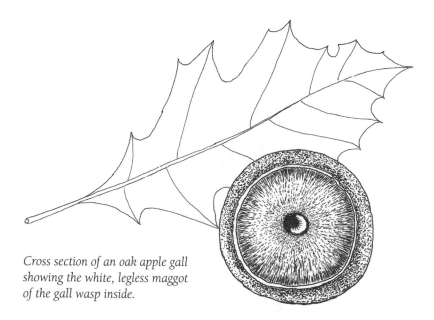

Cross section of an oak apple gall showing the white, legless maggot of the gall wasp inside.

smooth, rough, bumpy, prickly, velvety, or hairy? Are they hard, woody, succulent (having fleshy tissue, like a cactus), or rubbery? Can you crush them with your hand? Write your observations in your field notebook.

Gall insects account for an enormous amount of the protein that birds, bats, squirrels, chipmunks, mice, and other animals use for food. Can you find any evidence that animals have been chewing or gnawing on the galls?

Collect a variety of galls from a variety of plants and cut them in half. Observe their design and make drawings or take photographs of them. What similarities and differences do you observe?

Insects in the Soil. Many insects overwinter in the soil and in plant material, where they find a safe haven from the cold and from predators. If snow does not completely cover the ground or is not too deep, you can find some of these insects to examine. You will need a trowel for digging and a bucket to hold the soil. A Burlese funnel, or insect strainer, is an effective tool for capturing insects that live in the soil or in decaying leaves. You need a fifty- to seventy-five-watt bulb, a wide-mouth funnel (you can make one from aluminum foil), some wire screening, a quart-size, wide-mouth jar, and enough rubbing alcohol to fill the jar to a level of about one and one-half to two inches. If you do not want to kill the insects, use water instead of the alcohol. (Some people add a thin layer of kerosene to prevent the alcohol from evaporating.)

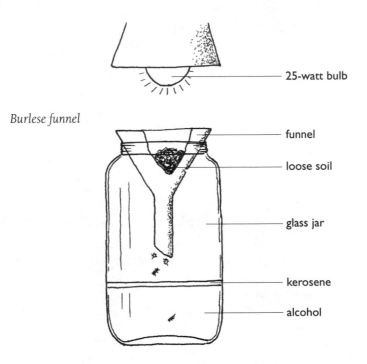

Burlese funnel

25-watt bulb

funnel

loose soil

glass jar

kerosene

alcohol

Cover the opening of the funnel with wire screening and put the funnel in the mouth of the jar. Pour in a handful, or about a half cup, of loosely packed soil or leaf litter. You may have to fluff the soil or litter a little or let it dry out somewhat if it is wet. Put the light source above the funnel to further dry out the soil. The insects in the soil will move down the funnel away from the heat toward moisture and tumble into the alcohol. Keep the light on for about six hours. If you don't find any insects, try again with soil from another place. Beneath a tree is a good place to find soil containing insects.

Examine the insects you have collected. How many different kinds did you trap? Do any have wings? Legs? How many? Do any of the insects look familiar to you? If you want to know what kind of insects they are, take your sample to a local nature center or your teacher for help in identifying them.

Repeat the procedure with samples of soil and leaf litter from different places, such as a wooded area, a field, and your backyard garden. Keep records of the insects you collect and where you found them.

Finding evidence of insects in the winter is not an easy task. With a little patience and willingness to spend some time poking around your neighborhood, you will find insects in various stages of their life cycle as they wait for the sun to return. Good luck!

CHAPTER 8

Birds

HOW THEY MEET WINTER'S CHALLENGE

A few years ago, winter delivered one of the worst ice storms in decades. When it was over, nearly everything in our corner of the world was covered with an icy glaze. The landscape was beautiful as it glistened in the January sunlight, but beneath the brittle beauty lay a harsh reality. Nesting cavities were ripped open as falling branches tore away the rotting wood beneath the tree bark. Seeds and berries usually available to birds were locked in ice. Owls and hawks had difficulty finding food in the frozen fields. Although each season brings a different set of problems for birds, winter poses the most difficult challenges.

During the millions of years that birds have been on earth, they have developed several strategies that help them survive the rigors of winter. One of these strategies is to migrate south from their northern breeding grounds to more hospitable lands. By late summer, birds that thrive on flying insects, such as orioles, flycatchers, thrushes, and warblers, are on their way south. Although their favored food is more readily available there, life in the land of sunshine has its own problems. The new arrivals must compete with native birds not only for a share of the bounty but also for territorial space in the rapidly diminishing woodlands and rain forests.

Birds that can find sufficient quantities of their preferred food remain in their northern breeding grounds throughout the cold months. Others that winter in the North simply change their diet. Instead of foraging for active insects, these birds find high-energy substitutes in such fare as dormant insects and seeds.

Sometimes there is not enough food in a region to support the huge numbers of birds that survive a very successful breeding season. Such a sudden population increase is known as an irruption. In response to this crisis, generally in late autumn, massive numbers of birds begin to flock into our northern states from Canada, where they have bred and where they usually spend the winter. It is not unusual for such birds to travel thousands of miles in search of scarce food.

Such movements by raptors like rough-legged hawks and snowy owls can be predicted because they are directly related to food supply, such as the number of lemmings available in the far north. At such times, snowy owls have been reported foraging on the beaches of Cape Cod and Long Island. Similar movements of northern shrikes depend on the abundance of mice in the birds' northern breeding grounds. Every three to five years the prey populations decline, and by November bird-watchers who live in the northern

rough-legged hawk

snowy owl

states such as Maine, Vermont, New Hampshire, New York, and Michigan report an increase in predaceous shrikes.

The mass movements of seed-eating birds are less predictable. They usually remain in their northern breeding grounds over the winter. Seeds from deciduous trees such as birch and aspen and the seed-laden cones of conifers normally sustain them throughout the winter. Movements of these birds into more southerly areas are difficult to predict because seed production depends on the vagaries of the weather—a warm spring and a warm autumn are necessary for a large crop of seeds. A bumper crop in one year does not mean a similar harvest the following year. In years of poor seed production, birds from the boreal forests descend across the Canadian border. At such times, residents of the northern states may see unusual winter visitors, such as redpolls, evening grosbeaks, pine grosbeaks, pine siskins, and red-breasted nuthatches, foraging with familiar winter birds such as cardinals, tufted titmice, and blue jays.

Migration and movements due to population surges are strategies for winter survival that are related to food supply. Except for those that migrate to tropical or semitropical climates, most birds must still cope with the frigid days and nights of winter.

Birds have evolved several strategies for surviving in cold weather. Some strategies cost very little in terms of energy use; others are extremely expensive. One of the least expensive survival techniques involves the birds' feathers. As the temperature goes down, birds fluff up their feathers through the workings of tiny muscles located in their skin. The fluffing action traps and holds the air surrounding the skin, which has been warmed by the birds' internal temperature (102 to 107 degrees F.).

northern cardinal fluffing its feathers on a cool winter day

Another, more expensive, strategy is to grow a more dense cover of feathers. Birds that winter in the cold climates have relatively more feathers than migrating birds. Tiny birds such as chickadees, kinglets, and creepers have more feathers relative to their size than the larger birds.

Most warm-blooded animals have devised a natual defense against life-threatening cold: They huddle. The smaller the animal, the more beneficial this strategy can be. Many birds use this strategy to keep warm, huddling together in trees, nest boxes, or any place where there is protection from ice storms or chilling winds. This roosting behavior helps minimize the difference between the body temperature of each bird and that of the surrounding air. When groups of birds huddle together, the heat lost from the group as a whole is similar to that lost from one large animal. Large animals have a smaller surface area relative to their size than smaller animals, thus they lose relatively less heat than smaller animals. The huddled "big bird" in the roost stays warmer than each of the little birds could if left alone in the cold. Scientists have learned that a cluster of house sparrows huddling in a nest box can save about 13 percent of the energy required to keep warm at night. Some birds, such as ruffed grouse and common redpolls, use the insulative properties of snow to protect them from the bone-chilling night air.

Shivering is another strategy birds use to keep warm. Because this method of getting warm has a high energy price tag, birds must eat large quantities of high-energy (high-fat-content) food to pay the debt. American goldfinches, for example, increase their body weight by 15 percent after a day of foraging. The payoff for the birds is that they can convert food into heat energy four to five times faster when shivering. They could not maintain the shivering if they had not eaten so vigorously. With their engines running at top speed, these birds can endure temperatures as low as minus 40 degrees F. The ability to increase their metabolic rate is believed to be triggered by the diminished light of winter. In the summer, when the days are longer, the birds can metabolize at such a high rate for only an hour. During the short days of winter, they may need to metabolize rapidly for many hours at a time.

Some birds use an opposite strategy, reducing their body temperature during periods of inactivity. When resting, chickadees can reduce their body temperature by about 50 degrees F., which slows their metabolism by 23 percent. This conservation strategy safely carries them through the night with sufficient reserve to fuel early-morning foraging activities. Hibernating animals usually have very low metabolic rates for long periods of time. Although we do not ordinarily associate hibernation with birds, poor-wills and possibly swifts are known hibernators in the bird world.

Most birds' legs are covered with scales, which do not protect from the cold. Those staying the winter in cold climates have shorter legs than their relatives living in warmer regions. This is a structural strategy that helps them conserve heat. Some birds have developed a protective behavior, frequently tucking one leg under the breast feathers to reduce heat loss. Look for these one-legged balls of feathers in trees and shrubs during the next cold spell.

Something called counter-current heat exchange also helps birds reduce heat loss through their legs and feet. It works in an interesting way. As in other animals, blood flows through arteries from a bird's heart to its extremities, while blood returning to the heart flows through veins. In birds' legs, arteries and veins are close to each other so that warm arterial blood passes some of its heat to the cooler blood in the veins. When the cooled arterial blood reaches the feet, considerably less heat is lost to the environment. In addition, this system decreases the potential shock to the birds' bodies from cold blood returning from the extremities.

A few winter-adapted birds have feathers that protect their legs from the cold. Ptarmigans wear feathered leggings and dense mats of stiff feathers on their feet. The legs of snowy owls are also sheathed in feathers.

Even with these adaptations for cold weather, mortality is high among birds that winter in cold climates. As many as 50 percent of chickadees wintering in the North do not live to sing the next spring. Scientists believe that many of these deaths are among the first-year birds, which may not have had access to good roosting sites or feeding grounds. Fierce winters are not as damaging to bird populations as are early freezes and unseasonable bad weather. Many strategies birds use to carry them through the winter are controlled by shorter days, so an early autumn can do as much damage as a severe winter.

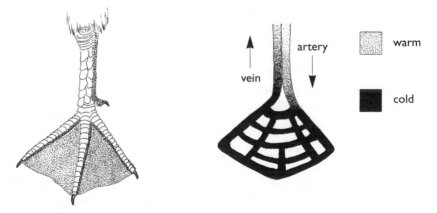

Counter-current heat exchange in the legs and feet of a mallard

In winter, ptarmigans grow stiff mats of feathers on their toes and thick feathered leggings.

If you live in Vermont, you may find that only about twenty species of birds spend the winter in your neighborhood, but if you live in Maryland, there may be over a hundred species. It is truly amazing that any of these tiny creatures can survive the low temperatures, snow, ice, and killing winds. Winter is certainly a challenge for birds.

THE WORLD OF WINTER BIRDS

What you will need	Science skills
basic kit	*observing*
camera	*recording*
field guide	*comparing*
birdseed	*inferring*
bird feeder	
patience	

OBSERVATIONS

Winter backyard birding has been going on for a long time. A 1985 survey indicated that more than 60 million people in the United States feed birds. You can join this group by putting a bird feeder in your yard.

The array of commercially available bird feeders can be confusing, because feeders come in a variety of styles and sizes. Some are cute, elaborate, and cleverly designed; others are simply utilitarian. Some feeders are so large they probably hold enough seed to feed all the birds at the National Zoo, and others are so small you would have to fill them almost hourly.

I like tube feeders with large plastic domes. The dome does a pretty good job of thwarting squirrels and it keeps the seed dry. Another favorite is the platform feeder. These are easy to build and allow a large number of birds to gather for a meal. Don't forget to clean your feeder regularly. A soapy scrub and a good rinse will do the job.

You can erect some feeders on posts and suspend others from tree limbs or a roof overhang. Others are designed so that you can affix them to windows.

Since squirrels also like seeds in their diet, you will probably find them eating up a storm at your feeder. Some people wage a constant battle trying to outwit them; others have found that squirrels will generally ignore feeders if you supply them with their own food. Ears of corn impaled on nails work well, or you can provide them with their own supply of seed. They don't seem to mind the inexpensive mixes. I like having squirrels around.

Build Your Own Feeder. You can make your own feeder from a two- or three-liter soda bottle and an inexpensive fitting designed especially for this kind of feeder, available at stores that sell bird feeders. The illustrations below show other types of low-cost feeders you can create to supply food for hungry birds.

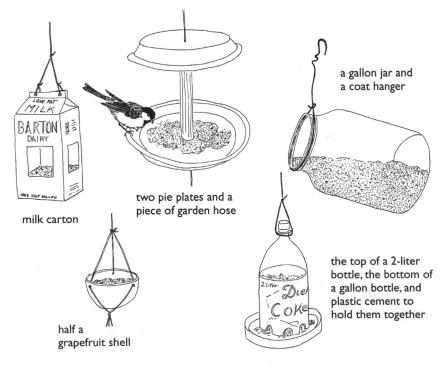

milk carton

two pie plates and a
piece of garden hose

a gallon jar and
a coat hanger

half a
grapefruit shell

the top of a 2-liter
bottle, the bottom of
a gallon bottle, and
plastic cement to
hold them together

Easy bird feeders

Seeds. Bird-watchers have discovered that you can attract different kinds of birds by using different types of seeds. If you want to have blue jays at your feeder, offer peanut kernels. Black-striped sunflower seeds will also attract these handsome birds as well as other seedeaters. Goldfinches' favorite food are hulled sunflower seeds. Thistle seeds, which require a special type of feeder, are enjoyed by goldfinches as well as pine siskins.

White proso millet scattered on the ground attracts ground feeders such as sparrows, juncos, and doves. Ground-feeding birds will also scurry around under your feeder cleaning up the seeds the other birds dropped.

Cracked corn and other grains will feed the gallinaceous birds, which include quail, pheasants, turkeys, and ptarmigans.

Set out a few feeders with different kinds of seeds and see what happens. Keep records so that you can deduce the favorite seeds of each visiting species.

To figure out how much seed you will need for the winter, you will need to determine how much seed, in pounds, it takes to fill your feeders and how long it takes for the birds to empty them. Do weather conditions (rain, snow, warm spells, or cold snaps) affect the amount of seed eaten? People who get a lot of birds can use hundreds of pounds of seed. One lady I read about uses between six hundred and eight hundred pounds of seed each year.

Suet. Technically, suet is the hard fat around the kidneys and loins of cattle. The term has been generalized to cover fat-based foods for bird feeding. The suet you buy at supermarkets, hardware stores, or other places that sell bird supplies is a high-energy food made of animal fat mixed with seeds and sometimes raisins or other fruits.

The plastic mesh bags that onions and some fruits are sold in are good to use for hanging suet from a tree limb or from the base of a hanging feeder. You can also buy sturdy wire mesh containers made to hold suet cakes. Secure these holders to tree trunks or hang them from some other place where you can observe the suet eaters. Look for woodpeckers, nuthatches, brown creepers, titmice, and chickadees. The suet "table" will quickly demonstrate to you that woodpeckers come in a variety of sizes and color patterns.

Feeding Behaviors. Sparrows, doves, and towhees prefer to eat at ground level, where they may be joined by quail, turkeys, and pheasants. Cardinals and jays prefer to eat at tabletop height, although they will forage on the ground if necessary. Goldfinches, chickadees, and tufted titmice are the birds that will come to hanging feeders. The suet cakes that you have attached to tree trunks will satisfy woodpeckers, creepers, and nuthatches. What other birds do you find feeding at these different levels, or niches?

Some birds feed in flocks; others are solitary feeders. Observe the birds

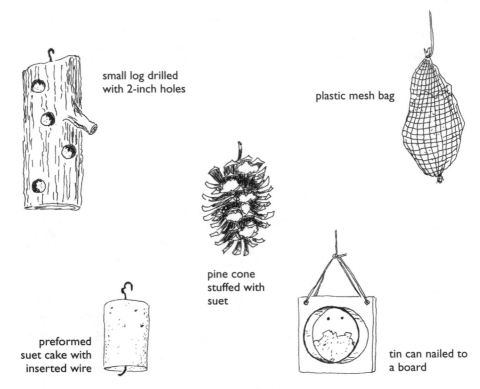

small log drilled
with 2-inch holes

plastic mesh bag

pine cone
stuffed with
suet

preformed
suet cake with
inserted wire

tin can nailed to
a board

Easy suet feeders

that feed by these two methods. What differences do you notice in the way the birds in these groups feed? What advantages, if any, does group feeding provide?

Water Source. It is important that the birds have a source of water available during the cold months. In some places, snow supplies this need. In regions where snow does not persist throughout the winter, the birds will look for other sources of water. Supplying ice-free water in a birdbath or other suitable container is a challenge, but there are electric birdbath heaters that will solve the problem. You can look for these in the stores that supply birdseed and feeders.

Identifying Birds. There are many excellent guides to bird identification from which to choose, and they are available in most bookstores. You will find some of the most widely used field guides listed in the Bibliography. If you are a beginner at bird identification, you might prefer to use a guide that covers only your region rather than a more inclusive guide that describes the birds that live in all of North America. Expert birders and teachers at nature centers can be extremely helpful to you as you sort through the large selection of available bird guides. As you become more proficient in bird identification, you may find that your first guide does not provide all of the information you would like to have at your fingertips. Seasoned birders own several field guides and use them regularly.

Once you have selected your field guide, read the introduction and skim through the rest of it. You will notice that the birds are grouped according to families. What kinds of information are given about the bird families? If the guide has range maps, what do the maps tell you? Why are the loons at the beginning of the guide and the passerine or perching birds at the back of the book? Get to know your guide; read through it whenever you have some extra time. The more you use your guide, the easier it will be for you to identify that mysterious bird that visits your feeder.

A good way to learn to identify birds is to go on bird walks. Look in your local newspaper for bird walks sponsored by a local bird club or a local chapter of the National Audubon Society. Nature centers and museums also sponsor walks.

The early stages of bird identification can be the most confusing and discouraging. This diagram of a bird will help you focus on the features that are commonly used to distinguish one kind of bird from another. Birders refer to these features as field marks.

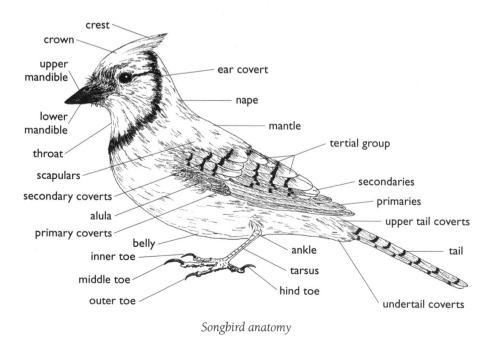

Songbird anatomy

Familiar bird silhouettes

Your first task when you see an unfamiliar bird at your feeder is to pay attention to the most general features of the bird—its size, shape, and color or color pattern. Next, observe specific details, such as the bird's bill, tail, head, wings, and feet. The bird's flight pattern can be another clue to its identity.

Size. Nearly everyone is familiar with the crow (seventeen to twenty-one inches), a robin (nine to eleven inches), and the sparrow (five to seven inches). These birds can be used as a mental measuring tape for determining the approximate size of your "mystery" bird. Is it smaller than a crow but bigger than a robin? Larger than a sparrow but smaller than a robin?

Shape. Birds can be plump or slender, chunky or sleek. What is the bird's general shape? Is it sleek like a crow? Chunky like a grosbeak? Stout like a nuthatch? Learning to recognize bird silhouettes against the gray of a winter sky or other drab background can be very helpful. Starlings, for example, differ from other birds of their size in that they have very short tails.

Color (Pattern). What color is the bird? Is there more than one color? Where are the colors? On the bird's back, breast, belly, rump, wings, or tail? Does it have wing bars? Does the color appear carelessly splashed on the bird, like the speckles on a starling? Or is it clearly defined, like the dignified black and white pattern of a hairy or downy woodpecker? A bird's name is often a reflection of its color. Blue jay, American goldfinch, purple finch, and redpoll are a few of the birds that sport their colors in their names.

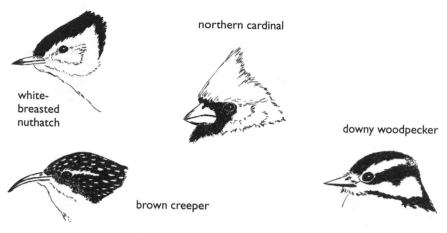

In general, the shape of the bill identifies the bird's family.

Bill. Generally, the shape of the bird's bill identifies the bird's family. Is the bill long or short, thick or slender, curved or straight? Is there anything unique about it? The crossbill's beak is twisted, making it effective in prying the seed from pine cones. You probably will not see these birds at your feeder, since they prefer to remain in the coniferous woods. Warblers have short, slender bills, but sparrows have short, thick bills. Warblers are primarily insect eaters, but the sparrows' thicker bills are good for cracking the hard coats of seeds. The curved bills of brown creepers are effective probing tools for picking out grubs from between the cracks in tree bark.

Tail. What is the shape? Color and pattern? Is it long like the tail of a mockingbird or short like the tail of a sparrow? Is it forked, notched, rounded,

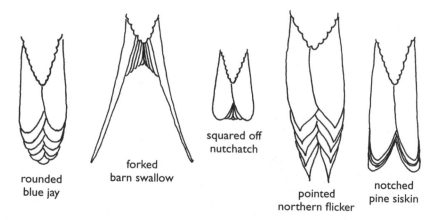

The shape of the tail is determined by the relative length of the tail feathers and is useful in field identification.

Carolina wren—
eye stripe

tufted titmouse—
eye rings

cardinal—
crest

chickadee—
black cap

or squared off? How does the bird hold its tail (see silhouette for shape)? Does the tail droop or is it held upright like a wren's? (The "tail up" image comes from the standard guidebook picture of a wren, but they often sing, a spring behavior, with tail pointed straight down.)

Head. What is the color? Is it a solid color or patterned? Are there eye stripes, as in a Carolina wren? Eye rings, as in a tufted titmouse or ruby-crowned kinglet? Does the bird have a crest like a cardinal? A hood or a cap like a chickadee?

Wings. Look for wing bars (thin lines) or wing patches of a lighter color than the wing. The wing bars or patches may have a dark margin that sets them off. The red-winged blackbird shows red wing patches with a yellowish margin when it flies.

Feet. The birds that visit backyard feeders are the perching birds and woodpeckers. The illustration show the difference in the feet of these two types of birds. How does the design of the feet help the birds when they eat? Compare the feet of the perching birds that come to the feeder with those of the woodpeckers that eat from the suet cakes affixed to the tree trunk.

perching bird foot

woodpecker foot

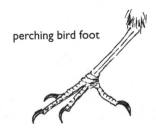

The feet of most woodpeckers have two toes pointing forward and two pointing backward, which helps anchor them as they chisel wood.

Passerine birds have a single hind toe, which helps them grip a branch when perching.

Finch flight

Most songbirds use bursts of flapping to gain altitude, followed by shallow dives with their wings closed.

Flight Pattern. Frequently birds will fly away from the feeder before you have an opportunity to get a good look at them, but you can get some information about the bird before it disappears. How does it fly? Does its flight pattern resemble a roller coaster, such as woodpeckers and finches? Does it flap, flap, glide? Does the bird fly in a straight line? It might be a mourning dove. Are the wingbeats slower than those of other birds? Perhaps your bird is the slow-flapping mockingbird. You might hear a whistle as the bird flies away. This tells you the bird is probably a mourning dove. Woodcocks also whistle as they take off, but you won't find these birds of moist woodlands and marshes at your feeder.

Certain birds will display additional colors and color patterns only when they are in flight. The slate-colored junco reveals white feathers on the outer margins of its tail when in flight. The towhee will show patches of white on the corners of its tail, and yellow-shafted flickers flash a white rump when in flight.

One Way to Begin. There are birds that are familiar to most people. When one of these familiar birds visits your feeder, observe it carefully. Make a list of the characteristics that helped you determine what it was. In doing this exercise, you will be applying the criteria needed to identify other birds. Try it. Learning to distinguish one bird from another takes patience, time, and more patience.

More Feeder Observations. At what time of the day do the birds first appear at your feeder? At what time do they stop coming? Is there a pattern to their eating? When do the peaks and valleys of feeding occur? Are they the same every day? What effect does the weather have on feeding?

Do certain birds come first, followed by other types of birds? At my feeder, the cardinals are frequently the first to show up in the morning and the last to feed in the late afternoon. Is this the case at your feeder?

EXPLORATIONS

Learning More about Your Favorite Bird. Many birders are fascinated with one kind of bird or group of birds and have made extensive studies of them. Is there a particular type of bird that visits your feeder that you would like to know more about? You can begin a study of this bird by observing its behavior and recording your observations in your field journal.

At what time of the day does the bird come to the feeder? Is it a solitary feeder or does it feed with other birds? Does the bird feed only with its own kind or does it feed with other kinds of birds? Does it eat the seed while at the feeder or does it take the seed and fly away? If it eats at the feeder, how does it open the seed? What other behaviors do you observe? While making your observations, you will probably answer some questions of your own. Record these in your field notebook.

Another step in learning about your bird of choice is to read about it. There are many fine books devoted to one kind of bird, and you can find these at your local library or obtain them through the interlibrary loan system. The staff at a local bird sanctuary or members of a local bird group also may be able to help you. When you have finished your research, write up a story about this bird that includes what you have learned. You may find that your local newspaper welcomes such stories about local birds written by a reader. A project such as this is fun to do with a friend. The following are some birds whose behavior you might like to explore:

1. Nuthatches. A suet feeder attached to a tree trunk will attract these small birds. Watch them for some fascinating behavior. Write a description of the bird as it works its way down the tree trunk. How does it hold its tail? Does it use the tail for support? How does it use its feet to prevent itself from tumbling to the ground? (See Chapter Note 1.)

2. Woodpeckers. Suet will also attract woodpeckers. Hairy and downy woodpeckers are frequent visitors to my suet cakes. You will need your guide book to help you figure out which is which between these two very similar birds. Which has the longer bill? How do these birds use their tails when eating from the suet or digging insects from the tree bark? How do their feet differ from those of the perching birds? What is the advantage of this design? (See Chapter Note 2.)

3. Goldfinches. The goldfinches at your winter feeder are not dressed in the bright yellow of spring. Use your field guide to determine whether the bird is a male or a female. If it is a male, when will he molt and get his bright-colored feathers? Do goldfinches feed in groups of other birds or are they solitary birds that prefer to eat alone? (See Chapter Note 3.)

white-breasted nuthatch

downy woodpecker

American goldfinch

A Successful Immigrant. The starling can teach you a lot about adaptations for survival. These birds were brought here from Europe during the early 1900s and have prospered in their new land. During the winter, starlings are easily recognized by the buff-white spots that dot their plumage. These spots are actually the tips of the birds' feathers.

Starlings forage in flocks. The number of birds in any one of these flocks can vary from ten to several hundred. Find some of these feeding flocks. About how many birds are there in each flock? What is the average number of birds in the flocks you found? There are advantages to foraging in flocks. Birds that feed in groups can spend more time feeding and less time on the lookout for predators. One researcher discovered that a bird feeding alone spends 50 percent of the time feeding and 50 percent looking around for predators. When five birds were in the feeding group, individuals could spend 70 percent of the time feeding. With ten birds in the flock, feeding time was 90 percent for each bird.

Observe a flock of starlings as they forage. They are not scattered haphazardly over the field, but there is an order to their activity. You may notice what some people have described as "leapfrogging." When the birds at the back of the flock are finished, they fly low over the flock toward the front. This rolling pattern is repeated throughout the feeding.

Late in the afternoon, while some of the pale light of the winter day remains, starlings leave their feeding grounds and congregate in larger groups. The places where these groups meet are called staging areas. Look for staging areas in your neighborhood. They could be in trees, on telephone wires, or on roofs of buildings. How many staging areas can you find? Sometimes these staging groups pick up additional birds as they fly to the roost. Did you see any of these airborne hitchhikers join the flock?

If you would like to learn some methods for estimating the number of birds in a flying flock, *The Audubon Society Handbook for Birders,* by Stephen W. Kress, gives some excellent suggestions.

Roosting Birds. Roosting is another strategy that protects the birds from predators and helps them keep warm during the cold winter nights. Roosts can be enormous, holding thousands to even tens of millions of birds, especially in winter roosts in the South. Starlings, red-winged blackbirds, common grackles, and brown-headed cowbirds make up about 98 percent of these flocks, but other blackbirds and robins may join them.

If you find birds roosting, you should not get too close to the roost area, because a secure roost is very important to the winter survival of the birds.

Scientists have discovered that dark-eyed juncos tend to roost in the same place night after night. Their roost is generally in a dense conifer or a grove of conifers. You can find out where the flock roosts by keeping track of where the birds go from the feeder. Follow them, but do not get too close. Look for the white feathers flashing as the birds flit among the branches before they settle down for the night. How many birds are in the roost? Juncos forage over a twelve-acre area, but the birds in the flock do not always feed together.

Short Days, Long Nights. Finding enough food to keep their internal fires burning throughout the long, cold winter nights is crucial for birds. How long is a winter night? Find the average number of daylight hours in the winter for your area. You can generally locate the information you need on the weather page of your local newspaper. How have some birds managed to get around the energy problem created by the short days of winter? (See Chapter Note 4.)

Adaptations for Feeding. Birds have adapted different strategies for getting food. A close look at bird beaks will give you some idea of the diversity of these strategies. The stout bills of the finches, grosbeaks, sparrows, and buntings (Fringillidae family) are powerful seed-cracking instruments. The beaks of crossbills, members of the same family, show a variation that's specifically designed to open pine cones and pick out the seeds inside. The hefty beaks of crows and jays (Corvidae family) are suitable for eating almost anything, which is what they do. The beaks of nuthatches (Sittidae family) allow a varied diet, including dormant insects found beneath tree bark as well as seeds.

Woodpeckers use another technique for getting food. Their long, sturdy, chisel-like bills are suited for digging holes in tree trunks to get at insects beneath the bark. Downy and hairy woodpeckers, red-headed woodpeckers, and red-bellied woodpeckers are among the common chiselers you can expect to see in your backyard.

Look for these different feeding adaptations in the birds that visit your backyard. In your field notebook, make drawings of the different kinds of beaks you see. Photographs are another excellent way to document your observations.

Bird Nests. You can expect to find abandoned bird nests in the winter, since they are no longer hidden by a thick curtain of leaves. Winter nests are usually vacant, but if you find one covered with leaves, it might be a temporary shelter for a mouse or some other weary traveler; do not disturb it.

Warning: It is against the law to take nests apart or to remove them from trees, shrubs, or any other place you may find them. You may, however, take photographs or make sketches of the nests in your field journal. Also write your observations in your journal. Include any questions you may have so that you can research them later.

Birds do not use their nests in the same way that we use our homes. For the birds, a nest is a place to lay their eggs, incubate them, feed the hatchlings, and serve as a jumping-off point when the young begin their flight lessons. After the young have learned to fly, the family breaks up, and for most bird species, the nest is no longer used. Some birds raise more than one brood in a season. These birds will build a new nest for each brood.

To find nests, search the trees and shrubs around your home and in your neighborhood. Walk along the edges of fields, look in thickets, on the ground, and in clearings. Look for dark clumps at various levels in the trees. Do not mistake the large, leafy summer nests (dreys) of squirrels for bird nests. When you spot a nest, record its location in your notebook. If the nest is in a tree, how high is it? Is it in the crotch of a limb, near the end of a branch, or close to the trunk? How many nests are there in the same tree? Include in your description the type of tree or shrub where the nest was found so that you can find it again.

Make a chart that shows the distribution of nests in your neighborhood. Have a friend make similar observations in his or her neighborhood and compare your charts.

About 77 percent of the birds in North America build open nests, and they come in a variety of sizes and shapes. The remaining birds raise their young in holes or in structures with rooflike tops. Blue jays prefer to build their bulky but well-hidden nests in conifers, generally ten to twenty-five feet off the

Robin's nests are steep cups made of grasses, weed stalks, and strips of cloth or string worked into wet mud and lined with soft grasses. They are built in shrubs, in tree forks, or on ledges.

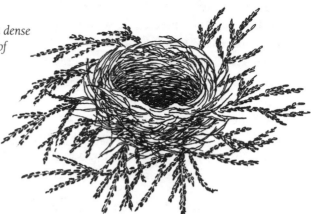

Cardinal's nests are built in dense shrubbery or brier tangles of loosely put together twigs, vines, grasses, and weed stalks. The nests are lined with fine grasses.

Sparrow nests are neatly cupped grass nests in low shrubs or on the ground.

ground. The nests are made of thorny twigs, bark, moss, string, and leaves. Robins build nests with weed stalks, strips of cloth, string, and grasses woven into soft mud. Robins and blue jays will build nests close to human habitation, so look for them in trees in neighborhood yards and along the roadside. Baltimore orioles build their pouchlike nests of plant fibers, hair, and yarn high in the trees, generally twenty-five to thirty feet above the ground. The rose-breasted grosbeak prefers to nest in moist, deciduous thickets and suburban trees and shrubs. It builds its flimsy nest of twigs six to twenty-five feet above the ground. The red-eye vireo's delicate nest of bark, grasses, vine tendrils, and paper is decorated on the outside with lichens. You can find these nests five to ten feet above the ground, suspended in the forked branches of saplings. Wood thrushes build compact nests of grasses, bark, moss, and paper, held together with mud. Their preferred sites are in deciduous trees, usually ten feet above the ground in parks or gardens. Wood thrushes appear to be growing more tolerant of human presence.

Because of the regulations against taking nests from the places where the birds built them, you may not have the opportunity to see many nests up close. Museums, nature centers, and other educational facilities may have

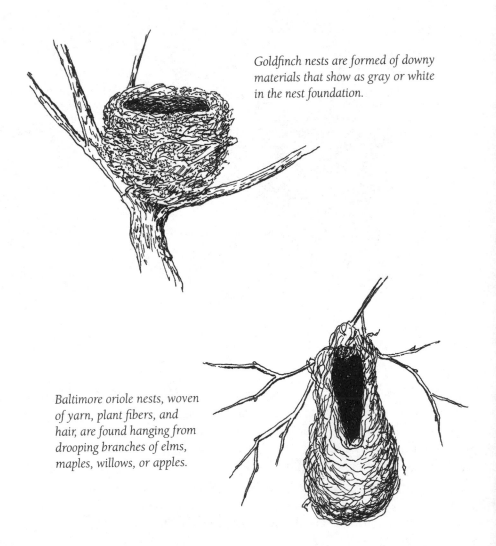

Goldfinch nests are formed of downy materials that show as gray or white in the nest foundation.

Baltimore oriole nests, woven of yarn, plant fibers, and hair, are found hanging from drooping branches of elms, maples, willows, or apples.

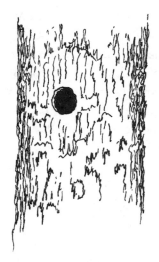

Chickadees, woodpeckers, titmice, nuthatches, and brown creepers nest in excavated cavities in dead trees.

collections of bird nests for you to examine. Compare those nests with the nests you found. What are the similarities and differences?

Take photographs wherever possible. You can add the photos to your field notebook or build a special notebook just for birds.

RESOURCES

1. Local chapters of the National Audubon Society are listed in the telephone book. If there is no listing for this group in your area, you can write to the national headquarters at 700 Broadway, New York, NY 10003, or call (212) 979-9009.

2. The Cornell Laboratory of Ornithology is a university-based education and field-research facility that has programs of interest for the general public. You can write to the facility at 159 Sapsucker Woods Rd., Ithaca, NY 14850, or call (607) 254-2400.

3. Bird rescue groups can be contacted through your local conservation officer, animal control center or the humane society.

4. The Bird Banding Laboratory, U.S. Fish and Wildlife Service, Laurel, MD 20708 will provide information about this activity that benefits both the birds and us.

CHAPTER NOTES

I. Nuthatches spiral down a tree trunk and dig from the crevices in the bark any insects they can find working from this vantage point. A close look at the birds' toes gives some clue as to how they keep their balance. Nuthatches do not use their short, flat tails to brace themselves against the tree trunk as woodpeckers do. In its characteristic pose, the nuthatch clings close to the trunk, beak pointed away from the tree, and supports itself only by its feet. Its toes are similar to those of perching birds—three toes in front and one in back. The difference, which you probably cannot see, even with binoculars, is that the back toe has a long claw that hooks into the bark of the tree.

Nuthatch beaks are not designed to crack nuts or acorns, a favored food. The birds jam acorns into the crevices of tree bark and peck them open with a series of strong jabs.

At the feeder, you might see it snatch a sunflower seed and fly off with it. The bird will either store the seed for a later meal or hammer it open for an immediate snack.

White-breasted nuthatches are the species you will usually see at feeders. A close cousin, the red-breasted nuthatch, prefers coniferous forests and favors pine seeds. If you live in the birds' winter feeding grounds and set your feeder near some conifers, you might have a visit from them.

2. Like the perching birds, most woodpeckers have four toes on each foot, but they are not arranged for perching or swimming. These birds have two toes facing front and two facing back. This is an ideal arrangement for supporting the bird while it hangs on to the trunk of the tree. One species, the three-toed woodpecker, has only one toe facing back but still manages quite well. When digging into the tree bark, the woodpecker also presses its long, stiff tail against the tree for additional support. This prevents it from seesawing when it pecks at the tree bark. Its specially designed skull prevents the bird from damaging its head while it pounds away at tree trunks with its sturdy bill. Its long tongue allows it to explore deep tunnels in tree trunks as it searches for the nuts and seeds stashed away by other birds. Woodpeckers generally don't harm trees; in fact, they provide a great service to the trees by eating many of the insects that do them harm.

3. Goldfinches will have their flashy feathers back by spring in time for the courtship season. The importance of the seasonal change in feathers goes beyond the mating rituals. Because the bird's life is not easy on feathers, a new set is a way to periodically remove worn-out feathers that could interfere with the bird's life. The goldfinch molt is typical of perching birds—slow and orderly. These birds do not lose all of their flight feathers at once, so while they are molting, they can still fly, unlike ducks, which lose all of their flight feathers at the same time.

Goldfinches are very social birds, so you can expect to see them at the feeder with other birds.

4. Pheasants, grouse, finches, and grosbeaks "eat" while they sleep. During the day, they pack a ration of seeds into a well-developed storage pouch called a crop. Then the seeds are slowly metabolized during the night, supplying sufficient energy for the sleeping bird, with a reserve to fuel early-morning foraging activities. Other birds, instead of storing seeds, lower their metabolic rate at night. This reduction of body processes is an effective strategy to conserve energy.

Many birds will take seeds from feeders to hoard them. Blue jays are among the best-known hoarders. Watch these birds stuff themselves while at the feeder, then fly off to hide the loot before returning for more. Red-headed woodpeckers store their bounty of nuts and seeds in the cracks of trees and fence posts. Nuthatches also store food, but their hiding place is beneath the loose patches of tree bark. The Clark's nutcracker, a West Coast relative of the blue jay, behaves in a similar way to its East Coast cousin. They both hide their supply of nuts and seeds and recover the food when needed. Their recovery rate is pretty good.

CHAPTER 9

Mammals

CREATURES *ARE* STIRRING

Winter is a time of hardship for most mammals. Food is scarce. Icy winds howl, snow falls, and the thermometer dips below freezing. One way we manage these harsh conditions is to warm our homes, pushing up the thermostat or adding an extra log on the fire. Our search for food is equally trouble free, involving only a short walk to the kitchen or, when the pantry is bare, a drive to the local grocery store, which provides us with easy access to the nutrients we need to fuel our internal fires. When we go to the supermarket in February, we can fill our carts with fruits and vegetables that were harvested in warm climates thousands of miles away.

Mammals that live in the wild do not have access to such technologies. In deep snow and bitter cold, they either survive or perish. They must rely on evolved strategies, but many of them die. Among black bears (*Ursus americanus*), however, there is an extremely good survival rate; only 1 or 2 percent of these shy, reclusive mammals die in any ordinary winter. How the bears manage the winter months has been the subject of scientific investigation for many years. These studies have revealed that black bears have developed complex strategies for coping with the cold season.

For a long time, people thought that the bears slept through the winter in cozy dens and in the spring emerged fully refreshed from their long snooze, but this is not actually the way the animals operate. In recent years, scientists have begun revising some long-held notions about hibernation and how the process works.

Hibernation is the mechanism that helps black bears conserve energy and reduce their internal fires to a mere flicker during the winter. Far from being a long, uninterrupted sleep, however, hibernation consists of periods of sleep punctuated by periods of arousal. Sleep time is long during the dead of winter but is shorter at the beginning and end of the season.

To pull off this metabolic trick, black bears must first add a huge amount of fat to their already large bodies. Through midsummer to the end of autumn, black bears feed ravenously, and scientists have figured out that they consume as many as twenty thousand calories in each twenty-hour day that they forage. The nutrients come from calorie-rich acorns, hazelnuts, and beechnuts and carbohydrate-laden blueberries, cherries, and wild sarsaparilla. If these preferred foods are in short supply, a feeding bear will eat whatever it can find. Bears are omnivores and will eat meat too, including roadkill and injured deer. By the end of the feeding period, a black bear will have added about five inches of body fat and more than doubled the insulation provided by its glossy black pelt. (See Chapter Note 1.)

As the bear enters the "sleeping" phase of hibernation, its metabolic processes such as body temperature, heart rate, and respiratory rate are reduced. With the help of technology, scientists now know that black bears do not lower their body temperature as much as was previously thought. With a hibernating temperature of about 88 degrees F., a sleeping bear needs to raise it only about 12 degrees to reach its waking temperature of 100 degrees F. This relatively high sleeping temperature allows black bears to become fully alert and able to protect themselves from predacious timber wolves and other dangers without unnecessarily taxing their energy reserves. Throughout the hibernating season, black bears will use approximately four thousand calories a day, resulting in a weight loss of about 20 percent.

Unlike black bears, which have been dubbed light sleepers, small mammals such as ground squirrels and chipmunks are deep sleepers. These little hibernators reduce their metabolic rates more drastically than black bears to help them get through the winter. The body temperature of the ground squirrel drops from 98 to 34 degrees F., and its heart rate shows a deep reduction, from 350 to a mere 2 beats per minute. Some of these small hibernators, like chipmunks, must wake up every few days to eat, which requires them to raise their body temperature. Unlike the bear, which stores reserve energy as body fat, these small deep sleepers get their nourishment from caches of nuts and seeds that they stashed away during the autumn harvest. Woodchucks also come close to a metabolic halt during the winter. This animal's heartbeat drops to less than twelve beats per minute, and its body temperature dips to a cool 37 degrees F. from a summertime high of 104 degrees F.

Black bears do not return to the same place year after year, nor do they hibernate in spacious caves. Cave dens are relatively small, measuring about seven feet deep and two feet high. The openings are just wide enough for a well-fed bear to squeeze through. Another surprise was that den sites are frequently open nests—shallow depressions the bears prepare for winter by lining them with bedding material such as pine and spruce branches and twigs, pieces of rotting wood, fibrous strips of cedar and other tree bark, chunks of moss, and leaf litter. Den sites also have been found in rock crevices and in hollow trees. A hole or depression left by an uprooted tree is also a suitable place for a black bear to spend the winter. The persistent root mass dangling from the felled tree provides a fine windbreak. Space in such a den is also only slightly larger than the denning bear. Sometimes bears just lie in the open and let the snow cover them. They have been known to lie in or under a brushpile with little advance preparation of the site.

By our standards, dens are not warm, and a bear with a low metabolic

A black bear in its den under a rock ledge.

rate cannot change that reality. In some dens, the temperature is only a few degrees higher than the soil. The bear's major protection from the cold comes from the insulative quality of its thick fur.

Bears enter their dens when signaled by an internal clock. Day length and regional weather patterns play an important role in the ticking of this clock, but the most vital role is played by food supply. What triggers the alarm to ring is still unclear, but it is probably safe to say that all bears have gone into their dens by the time there is a heavy snowfall in the region.

Black bears are generally solitary hibernators. An exception for this preference may be made if den sites are scarce. And when a female bear has cubs that were born during the previous winter, she will den with the cubs.

The mating period for black bears extends from May to July. Although it takes about three months for the embryo to develop, bear cubs are not born until January or February. The lapse of time between the fertilization of the egg and the birth of the cubs confounded scientists until they discovered an explanation for this mystery.

After the egg is fertilized and undergoes some cell divisions, development ceases. The tiny blastula, or ball of cells, remains suspended in the uterus until the autumn. At that time, the modified blastula, now called a blastocyst, implants itself in the wall of the uterus, where growth continues until a fully developed cub is born. Scientists call this interruption in development embryonic delay, and it is a survival advantage to the mother and the cubs alike.

Without embryonic delay, black bear cubs would be born during the summer months. This would be a dangerous time for them, because then the mother bear is concerned with her own survival. She instinctively knows she must put on sufficient body fat to make it through the winter, and newborn cubs would be a secondary consideration for her. Because a female black bear can produce between one and five cubs every two years, she is very valuable to the species, and this mating-birth cycle protects her.

At birth, the cubs weigh about one-half to three-quarters of a pound. They are blind, naked, and completely dependent on their mother. They know instinctively to snuggle close to her, finding warmth from her breath as they nestle in the folds of her fur. The lactating mother offers the cubs milk, which is approximately 25 percent fat (human milk is 4 percent fat), even though she may sleep as she did through the birth process.

As longer days signal the coming of spring, the mother and her cubs prepare to leave the den. In the coming months, the cubs become less dependent on their mother and the milk she provides. By the age of six months, bear cubs are weaned and can fend for themselves if necessary. Usually mother and cubs will den up for the winter following an autumn of foraging, and it is not unusual for the cubs to remain with their mother for two years. This extended intimacy enhances the cubs' chances for survival. They learn how to forage, how to find suitable den sites, and how to ward off predators, including humans.

Black bears are revealing a great deal about themselves as scientists continue to study them. The results of some studies have implications for us. Although the bears spend long periods of time lying down, they do not exhibit bone degeneration due to calcium loss as do humans when confined to bed. Black bears do not suffer from gallstones because they produce a chemical that prevents their formation. Even though bears thrive on their own body fat and have high blood cholesterol levels, they are free from the cardiovascular diseases that plague our population.

As the human population continues to increase, housing developments and recreational facilities spill into wild animal habitats. Conflicts with those animals are inevitable. With careful planning, however, wildlife biologists tell us we can live in harmony with those shy, reclusive symbols of the wilderness, black bears.

THE WINTER WORLD OF MAMMALS

What you will need

basic kit

camera

sketchpad

tape measure

tracking guidebook

dedication

Science skills

observing

comparing

inferring

classifying

OBSERVATIONS

What a thrill it is to see a moose along a highway in Maine or an elk in Montana, or even a few browsing deer in almost any rural area. These are rare experiences, because most wild mammals are careful to avoid humans. Even in summer, the smaller mammals like beavers, raccoons, skunks, otters, and opossums are seldom seen unless they blunder into the path of an automobile. During the winter, these mammals are even more difficult to observe.

Many mammals remain hidden in dens, burrows, or tree cavities during the most severe periods of the winter. Those that do wander in search of food do so in the shadowy predawn hours or at dusk. The dim light coupled with the protective coloration of the animals' fur hide them from all but the sharpest eyes.

Although we usually do not see these animals, we can learn of their presence through the signatures they leave on the snow-covered landscape. The paws and hooves of animals make impressions in the snow, known as tracks, or prints. A series of prints makes a trail. Other signatures include droppings, or scat, toothmarks left on broken twigs, and clawmarks on the bark of trees. These visible clues alert us to the presence of the very shy mammals that are active in our neighborhoods throughout the winter. In the following activities, you will have an opportunity to peek into the private lives of those animals. Refer to the books listed in the Bibliography to learn more about the animals that visit your neighborhood. (See Chapter Note 2.)

The Feet That Make the Prints. Through the evolutionary history of mammals, two basic foot types have developed. One type is the cloven hoof of deer, moose, cows, pigs, and goats. The print left by a cloven hoof shows two elongated toes of equal length. If the snow is deep enough, you will see the print of a deer's dew claw, which is located higher on the leg than the dog's dew

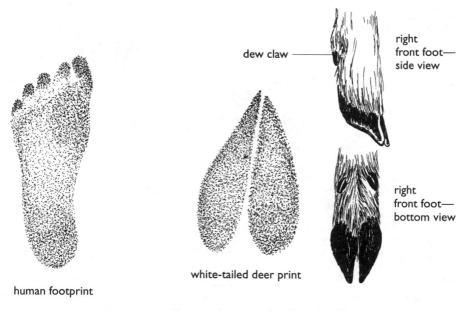

right
front foot—
side view

dew claw

right
front foot—
bottom view

white-tailed deer print

human footprint

Comparison of human footprint to a cloven hoofprint

claw. Dew claws also show when deer run. The more complex feet of other mammals resemble our feet in that they have toes, insteps, and heels.

When mammals travel in the snow, they leave a series of prints. These prints, or tracks, provide us with some information about that animal: the direction in which it is going, what it may have been doing, whether it was traveling alone or with others of its own kind. We can sometimes also see from where the tracks lead whether the animal browsed on vegetation or left clawmarks on tree trunks.

Dogs. A way to begin exploring your neighborhood for animal tracks is to first examine the front and hind feet of a friendly dog. The black pads you see on the bottom of the dog's foot are shock absorbers for the dog when jumping and provide friction when running. Feel them. Describe their texture. How many pads are there on the front foot? Are they all the same shape? Describe their shapes. What is the relationship between the toes and pads? Do the claws grow beyond the tips of the pads? Compare your nails with those of a dog. How are they different? Compare the front and hind paws and the front and back legs of the dog. How are they similar and how are they different? Write your observations in your field notebook.

Dogs and other members of the canid group of mammals, such as wolves,

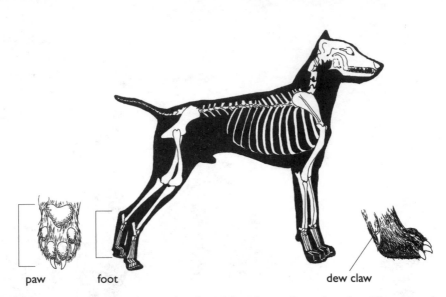

paw   foot

dew claw

If we compare dogs' feet to human hands and feet, dogs walk on their four "fingers" and toes. On the front foot, they have a fifth toe called the dew claw an inch or so up the inside of the leg; this is equivalent to the human thumb.

coyotes, and foxes, walk on their toes. These animals have four toes that generally leave their mark in the snow. The fifth toe, or dew claw, on each front paw, about an inch or so up the inside of the leg, is analogous to our thumb. Unlike our very valuable thumbs, however, the dew claws do not have much practical use, except that wild canids use them to grasp large prey. The dew claws will sometimes show up in the track if the animal is in a high-speed gallop.

Typical domestic dog tracks have an overall round appearance, especially the larger front track, where the four toes splay outward in different directions.

The prints made by all members of the canid group have similar characteristics. Both front and rear paws usually will show four claws and four toe pads, one behind each claw. Each print will be longer than it is wide. The next time there is a fresh cover of snow, walk around your neighborhood— along sidewalks, through backyards (get permission from the owners), park lawns, school grounds, public golf courses, and fields—and look for dog prints. When you find a set of tracks, determine how many dogs there were and in what direction the dog or dogs were traveling. How many different sets of prints did you find on your walk? Measure the length and width of a print in each set. What was the range in size (length and width) of local dog prints?

Cats. Another neighborhood animal is the domestic cat. Although much smaller in size, these cats belong to the same family of mammals (Felidae) as the bobcat, tiger, lion, and leopard. If you don't own a cat, ask a friend if you may examine the paws of his or her cat. Look at the claws and pads. Compare these structures with those you found on the dog. How are they similar and how are they different? Would you expect to find clawmarks in a print left by a cat? Explain your answer. (See Chapter Note 3.) Does a cat also walk on its toes? What is the general shape of a cat's paw? How does its shape differ from that of a dog? The print left in the snow by a domestic cat is very similar to but smaller than those left by bobcats or other larger cats in the wild. A round, clawless print is a clue that it was made by a feline.

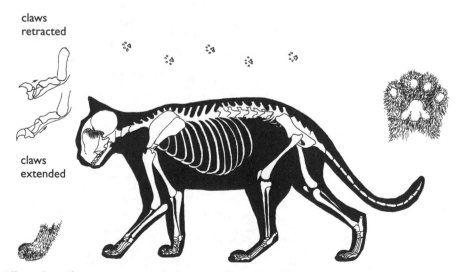

All cats have four toes in a circular print, with no claws showing. Large, protruding cheekbones, forward-facing eye sockets, and a short muzzle give the cat a round, flat face.

Identifying Animal Tracks. The chart below will help you focus on some of the characteristics of tracks and trails. The length and width of a track are clues to help you decide which animal made the print. Different books or teachers use different measuring techniques, so if you are using a tracking book as a guide, you need to make sure you are measuring the tracks using the same method as described in the guide.

When taking measurements of prints, you will need to measure more than one track. After snow has fallen, it is affected by the environment, and prints or tracks made in it will change in appearance. Those you find in freshly fallen snow will look very different from those you find in slushy snow. You can discover this for yourself by making some footprints of your own in freshly fallen snow. Examine your prints the next day. How have they changed?

ANIMAL TRACKS

Mammal	Prints	Facts
Deer		Two large toes create a heart-shaped cloven hoof, with dew claws just above the hoof. In deep snow, dew claws will be part of the track. Tracks measure $1\frac{1}{2}$ to $3\frac{1}{2}$ inches long by $1\frac{3}{8}$ to $2\frac{7}{8}$ inches wide.
Dog		Four toes, front and rear. The claws usually show. Prints generally longer than wide. Size varies with breed.
Cat		No claws in print. Circular print with four toes. Size varies with breed. Cats generally go directly from walk to gallop; they can trot but usually do not.
Eastern cottontail		Four toes often indistinct on front and hind feet. Front tracks oval 1 inch long, hind tracks oval 3 inches long. Usually hop; trail often zigzag.

ANIMAL TRACKS

Mammal	Prints	Facts
Gray squirrel		Five toes on hind feet, four on front feet. Hind track 1 inch wide by 2¼ to 2½ inches long if whole foot shows. Active in the daytime. Print looks similar to eastern cottontail's, except that tracks from squirrel's two front feet are generally side by side.
Striped skunk		Five elongated toe pads with claw marks, but frequently little toe doesn't show. Front print 1⅞ inches long by 2³⁄₁₆ inches wide, including nails and heel. Hind prints show entire foot, similar to human foot. Print is delicate.
Raccoon		Five long, fingerlike toes. Front print 2 to 3 inches long by 1⅞ to 2½ inches wide; hind print 2⅜ inches wide by 3¾ inches long. Track shows widely spaced toes.
Opossum	 not to scale	Five long, fingerlike toes on front track. Front track 1½ to 2⅛ inches long by 1¾ to 2⅜ inches wide; rear track 1¾ to 2¾ inches long by 1¾ to 2⅞ inches wide. Hind track has thumblike appendage that's useful for grasping

Keep a record of the animal tracks and trails you find in your neighborhood. Include a drawing, the date, weather conditions, time of day, type of animal, and comments.

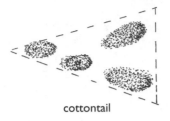

cottontail   squirrel

The cottontail tracks on the left show the common triangular pattern of the rabbit family. The squirrel's front feet are side by side.

RECORD OF TRACKS

Date	Illustration	Weather	Time	Type of Animal	Comments
a.					
b.					
c.					

Other Signs. In addition to tracks, animals leave other signs on the winter landscape that indicate their presence. As you become accustomed to exploring the world of winter, these other signs will become more obvious to you. They may include the animals' scat, or droppings, evidence of browsing, or packed pathways in the snow. The following is a brief outline of signs that some common animals that may winter in your area generally leave behind.

white-tailed deer

THE LIFE

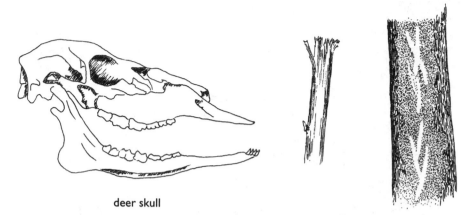

deer skull

Deer have no upper incisors, so when they browse, they leave rough, torn, or squared-off cuts. They also scrape bark from different trees for food, using an upward motion. They leave incisor marks on the stripped trees.

White-Tailed Deer (*Odocoileus virginianus*). Because deer lack incisors (those front teeth that nip and snip) on the upper jaw, the twigs they chew look torn and ragged. Rabbits, on the other hand, have incisors and make clean forty-five-degree-angle cuts on twigs. Look for deer browse at a height somewhere between your knee and hip. This height will vary with the depth of the snowpack. Deer also scrape bark from trees with their lower incisors. Look for scrape marks on hemlock, sumac, willow, witch hazel, mountain ash, shadbush, alder, cherry, and apple trees.

Deer seek shelter in areas protected from the weather by hemlock, pine, and spruce trees. These areas are called yards, and they can be huge, covering many, many acres with hundreds and even thousands of deer. Deer yards are larger in the northern part of deer range and smaller to the south. Deer runs are paths of packed snow that lead to feeding or bedding areas. Packed snow makes it easier for the deer to travel.

Winter whitetail droppings, or scat, are easy to recognize. They are cylindrical pellets with one pointed end and are generally under an inch in size.

When walking, the red fox leaves a straight, narrow line of tracks, where the hind track registers directly on top of the front.

Red Fox (*Vulpes vulpes*). Widely distributed throughout North America, these wary creatures prefer to live closer to us than most people think. They appear in the suburbs and in rural areas but avoid the wilderness. Tracks and scat are among the many clues they leave behind. The red fox usually has reddish fur and a white-tipped tail. These animals may also be black or silver, but the white-tipped tail is a clue to their true identity.

Red foxes bed down in open fields or on south-facing slopes in mountainous or hilly areas. They construct a series of pathways that mark areas of intensive use. Their path through the snow is usually a straight line, unlike the meandering track of the well-fed domestic dog. Look for red foxes in fields, mixed woodlands, and even suburban backyards. Abundant food is the drawing card. Red fox diet includes small mammals, insects, and carrion.

Scat reflects the animals' diet. You can expect to find it filled with hair from small animals such as voles, mice, chipmunks, and squirrels. You may also find small bones, ranging in size from two to four inches long and about

dog scat (size varies with breed)   **fox scat**

In winter and spring, fox scat is composed mostly of hair and often has pointed ends.

one-half inch in diameter. Of the two measurements, diameter is the most significant, because length can vary considerably. Red fox scat has a musky odor that aids in its identity.

Eastern Cottontail (*Sylvilagus floridanus*). Two pairs of upper incisors, one behind the other, plus lower incisors make these mammals efficient at gnawing. Look for the clean forty-five-degree cuts on twigs that suggest rabbits were feeding there. Cottontails browse on sumac, maple, apple, blackberry, and oak. They prefer farmland, pastures, hedgerows, and dense thickets where they can hide. These rabbits do not dig burrows, but they may escape danger by darting into abandoned skunk or woodchuck holes.

Their scat is in the form of small (half-inch-diameter), light brown, flattened spheres that resemble sawdust. Since rabbits drop these pellets one at a time, a heap of them indicates that the rabbit spent some time in that particular place.

eastern cottontail

Rabbits have sharp top and bottom incisors, creating a clean 45° cut when they browse.

In fall and winter, cottontails gnaw the bark of fruit trees. The scattered scats also mark cottontail feeding places.

Eastern Gray Squirrel *(Sciurus carolinensis)*. A squirrel's winter home is often the dry hollow of an abandoned tree hole. Look for these nests, especially in oak or beech trees. The nest is lined with grass, moss, and shredded leaves. Dreys, large loose bundles of leaves firmly anchored in the crotch of a tree, serve as summer nests. Squirrels often raise a second litter in them. Look for them in the naked deciduous trees of winter.

Gray squirrels prefer acorns and other large nuts to hemlock or pine seeds. They do not store underground caches of nuts, although they bury a great many nuts individually each fall. Although squirrels don't always remember where they stashed them, retrieval of many is possible because of the animals' excellent sense of smell. Those nuts left behind often germinate and grow to trees. Squirrels thus plant many trees, including black walnut, butternut, beech, oak, and hickory, throughout our parks and forests. Gray squirrel population is directly proportional to the number of nuts produced on each squirrel's home range.

gray squirrel

Telltale signs of the gray squirrel—nibbled pine cones, acorns, and hickory nuts, along with squirrel scat.

Squirrel droppings are oval and smooth. Because squirrels are regularly found around bird feeders, you can expect to find their scat nearby.

Striped Skunk (*Mephitis mephitis*). You will see signs of this member of the weasel family in suburban neighborhoods. Even in rural areas, there are indications of their presence close to our homes and especially close to garbage pails. Skunks are light sleepers, and their slightly slowed metabolism quickly rises to normal rates during warmer periods throughout the winter. Rising temperatures and decreasing snow cover are factors that contribute to the skunks' resumed periodic activity. Early in the spring, the desire to mate is an additional factor that contributes to the skunks' renewed activity. You can expect to find them ambling through your neighborhood after dark in search of food. Other members of the family are the fisher, weasel, otter, mink, badger, and marten.

All members of the weasel family have five toes on their front and back feet. Frequently you can find delicate skunk tracks going in and out of holes in the ground where the animal has been snoozing during the harsh weather. Skunks waddle.

Striped skunks like to den in tree crevices or beneath buildings, but their favorite spots are underground dens abandoned by other animals. Skunks are especially fond of those dens made by woodchucks. Dried leaves and grasses scattered around the opening are a good indication of a skunk's presence.

striped skunk

Striped skunk scat is usually black and much bigger than you might think. It may reach ¾ inch or more in diameter.

Skunks are omnivores, but their scat is almost always composed of insect parts. If the skunk has been feeding on berries or small animals, the scat will contain seeds and bits of hair. Scat, which is black and three-quarters of an inch in diameter, is usually found in feeding areas, although you may find it anywhere the animals roam.

Raccoon (*Procyon lotor*). Most raccoons mate between January and March, but those living in colder regions begin mating somewhat later than raccoons that live in the South. Most litters are born in April, but those kits that were conceived late in the breeding season won't arrive until midsummer. These latecomers born in the North frequently cannot store enough fat to sustain them throughout the long northern winter; as you might expect, their late-arriving southern cousins have a better survival rate.

typical raccoon

Throughout the cold months, raccoons maintain most of their normal body processes and spend much of the time alternating between sleep and wakefulness. During periods of extreme cold, they are not active. Early in the season, they rarely venture out if the temperature is below 30 degrees F. Later, however, it is not unusual for raccoons to be out on nights when the mercury drops to a few degrees above zero. Toward the end of the winter, raccoons spend more time away from their dens looking for food. Unfortunately, many foraging raccoons are killed by vehicles on the roads.

Raccoons prefer to live in and around wetlands such as marshes, swamps, and streams, but these highly adaptable creatures also thrive in cities and suburbs where their natural habitats have been destroyed. They frequently find shelter in the hollows of hardwood trees such as basswood, maple, sycamore, beech, oak, and sweet gum, but since raccoons are very adaptable, you can also find them living comfortably in abandoned wood duck boxes, empty woodchuck burrows, sewer conduits, and church steeples. They will even share lodging with other living things in barns, garages, sheds, and houses.

The raccoon's front paws make a roundish print with five long toes. They are frequently compared to a human hand in miniature. The tracks of the hind paws are longer but also have five toes.

Raccoons generally make latrines along the pathways of ordinary travel. Look for their scat scattered around the bases of the trees that are not den sites, on top of stone walls, or in forks of trees close to the ground. The droppings vary in appearance but generally are flat ended. Because raccoons are omnivores, you can expect to find seeds, insects, fur, and remains from neighborhood garbage pails incorporated into their scat. Raccoons in certain areas carry roundworms in their intestinal tract, so it is not wise to touch scat if you think it might be from a raccoon.

Raccoon scat is large, crumbly, and flat ended.

THE LIFE

opossum

Opossum (*Didelphis virginiana*). The opossum is one of our most misunderstood nocturnal mammals. Unfortunately, the only opossums most people ever see are the frequent roadkills. Found throughout the United States and southern Canada, these shy animals usually avoid human observation even though they live in our backyards. The opossum has a long, pointed face with pink snout; beady eyes; pale, gray-white fur that's often tinged with a wash of yellow; and a hairless, ratlike tail covered with scales.

Opossums are among the most silent animals that live in the North American woodlands, but when frightened or threatened they growl and hiss. Even though opossums will snap their jaws and flash fifty needle-sharp teeth that can cause a painful wound, this may seem like meager protection when compared with the protective armor of the turtle, the spearlike quills of the porcupine, or the repulsive odor of the skunk. They also lack the speed to outrun such predators as foxes, wolves, and bobcats. Nevertheless, opossums are skilled at some very effective survival techniques.

Opossums are superb climbers. Each hind foot has an opposable toe, or thumb, which allows it to grasp objects. It can't press the thumb pad closed against its other fingers, however, so it's not able to pick up small things such as seeds. Opossums also have a highly maneuverable tail, which allows them

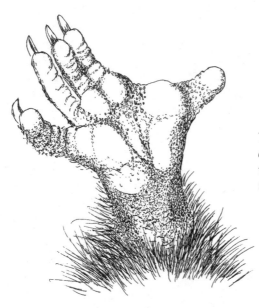

The right hind foot of the opossum. Note the "thumb," which permits the opossum to grasp objects.

to move through the trees with an astonishing agility. Once safely above the ground, an opossum can disappear into a tree cavity and remain there until the danger has passed.

Opossums have another neat trick for avoiding trouble; they feign death. To do this, the animal lies on its side, stiff and seemingly lifeless, its eyes half closed and mouth open with tongue hanging out. It even smells dead, thanks to an odoriferous liquid excreted by a pair of anal glands. An opossum can play dead for several hours if necessary, not moving a muscle even if poked, bitten, kicked, or picked up and dropped with a thump. Scientists are unsure why opossums use this prey-avoidance strategy or exactly what happens to them when they play dead. Recent study of opossum brain waves has shown

Opossum scat is not usually found. Some observers believe that opossums digest their food so well that their scat is seldom solid and thus disintegrates quickly.

that the animals do not hypnotize themselves into a stupor or experience a paralytic seizure, as was once thought.

The opossum has five toes on each front and hind paw that splay or spread out when the animal puts weight on its toes. Like many other mammals, the hind paws are placed next to or partially over the front track when walking. The hind print is distinctive because of the presence of the opposable thumb.

Although opossums live quite well in tree hollows and other natural places, they also find shelter in the basements, garages, barns, sheds, and porches that we have graciously provided. Good shelter is especially important for opossums, since they spend so much energy and time reproducing.

It is difficult, even for the experts, to distinguish opossum scat from that of other mammals of similar size.

Looking for the signs of these animals in your neighborhood can be fun, but to become skilled, you will need to work with an experienced tracker over a period of many months. The books listed in the Bibliography are considered among the best in the field. I hope you will take the opportunity to explore the tracks and trails of the variety of animals that appear when snow covers the ground.

CHAPTER NOTES

1. According to *Walker's Mammals of the World*, female bears weigh from 180 to 280 pounds and males 230 to 540 pounds. Bears reach their maximum weight just before they go into their dens for the winter.

2. A great deal can be discovered about the mammals that live in your neighborhood by investigating their tracks, but you should remember that any print will vary considerably from the standard illustration found in introductory books when the tracks are left in wet sand or mud. The prints left in fresh, fluffy snow also will look different from the tracks seen in old or icy snow.

3. The cat is a silent stalker, a characteristic that is very useful to predators whose rodent prey have especially keen hearing. The secret of this silence lies in the design of the cat's paws. If you examine the paws of a friendly cat you will notice that there are five toes on each front foot and four toes on each back foot. Each toe is made up of three bones that are similar to the bones of your fingers and toes. At the end of each toe is a claw that is covered by skin when the cat's paw is relaxed. It is the ability to retract or pull in its claws that allows it to walk quietly.

You can cause the cat to extend its claws. First put a toe pad between your thumb and index finger at the joint between the first and second toe bone, then gently squeeze your fingers. Look for the claw and the first bone to extend. Cats can retract or extend their claws as they need to through the interaction of muscles, tendons, and ligaments.

Toenails clicking on the bare floor announce the presence of a dog. Compare the cat's paws with those of your favorite canine and you can see why dogs are not good silent hunters.

Selected Bibliography

I. THE SCENE

Berman, Bob. *Secrets of the Night Sky.* New York: William Morrow and Company, 1995.

Cvancars, Alan M. *Exploring Nature in Winter.* New York: Walker and Company, 1992.

Halfpenny, James C., and Roy Douglas Ozanne. *Winter: An Ecological Approach.* Boulder, CO: Johnson Books, 1989.

Jobb, Jamie. *The Night Sky Book. An Everyday Guide to Every Night.* Boston: Little, Brown and Company, 1977.

Marchand, Peter J. *Life in the Cold: An Introduction to Winter Ecology.* Hanover, NH: University Press of New England, 1991.

Pasachoff, Jay M., and Donald H. Menzel. *A Field Guide to the Stars and Planets.* New York: Houghton Mifflin Company, 1992.

Zim, Herbert, and Robert H. Baker. *Stars: A Golden Guide.* New York: Golden Press, 1972.

II. THE LIFE

Borror, Donald J., and Richard E. White. *A Field Guide to the Insects.* Boston: Houghton Mifflin, 1970.

Brockman, Frank. *Trees of North America.* New York: Golden Press, 1976.

Brown, Lauren. *Weeds in Winter.* Boston: Houghton Mifflin Company, 1976.

Buff, Sheila. *Birding for Beginners.* New York: Lyons & Burford, Publishers, 1993.

Burt, William H. and Richard P. Grossenheider. *A Field Guide to the Mammals.* Boston: H

Connor, Jack. ...ton: Houghton Mifflin, 19

Ehrlich, Paul, ...'s Handbook: A Field Guide ...ds. New York: Simon and

Garland, Trud ...Numbers. Palo Alto, CA:

Halfpenny, Jar ...erica. Boulder, CO: Johns

Imes, Rick. *Th ...huster, 1992.

Kress, Stephe ...rs. New York: Charles S

Martin, Alexar ...llife and Plants: A Guide to ...cations, 1951.

Murie, Olaus ...ghton Mifflin, 1974.

Newcomb, La ...and Company, 1987.

Peterson, Rog ...ghton Mifflin, 1980.

Petrides, Geor ...)88.

Rezendes, Pau ...Camden House Publishing

Robbins, Char ...uide to Identification: Birds of North America.* New York: Golden Press, 1983.

Stokes, Donald. *A Guide to Nature in Winter.* New York: Little, Brown and Company, 1976.

————. *A Guide to Observing Insect Lives.* Boston: Little, Brown and Company, 1983.

Trelease, William. *Winter Botany.* New York: Dover Publications, 1976.